ACTA UNIVERSITATIS UPSALIENSIS
Studia Anglistica Upsaliensia
30

Catarina Ericson-Roos

The Songs of Robert Burns
A Study of the Unity of Poetry and Music

Uppsala 1977
Distributor: Almqvist & Wiksell International,
Stockholm, Sweden

Doctoral dissertation at the University of Uppsala 1977

ISBN 91—554—0576—2
ISSN 0562—2719

Printed in Sweden by
Borgströms Tryckeri AB, Motala, 1977

Phototypesetting by
TEXTgruppen i Uppsala ab

Contents

Acknowledgements

Many people have given me aid and assistance in the course of this study. I first wish to thank my supervisor, Dr. Ann-Mari Hedbäck, for her continuous support, her constructive criticism and for the meticulous care with which she has gone through every stage of this work. Professor Gunnar Sorelius, who read the manuscript at every major stage, has been most generous with both time and understanding. His suggestions, keen observations and interest have been invaluable. Professor Cedric Thorpe Davie, University of St. Andrews, read the whole manuscript, gave critical comments, suggested many stylistic improvements and kindly received me for a discussion on musical matters. But I especially wish to thank him for all his encouragement which has been much needed at various stages. I have also profited greatly from the advice and illuminating comments of Dr. Thomas Crawford, University of Aberdeen, who was most hospitable when I visited him. The discussions I had with him proved to be an immense source of inspiration. Mr. Peter Cooke, at the School of Scottish Studies in Edinburgh, read early drafts, and his expert advice and elucidating comments on ethnomusicological matters have been invaluable. Mr. Hamish Henderson, also at the School of Scottish Studies, inspired my interest in Scottish folk-songs in general through his lectures on this subject, and through his spontaneous and positive reaction to some early chapters I felt encouraged to go on. I also owe a great debt to Mrs. Linda Headlee, who opened up the doors to Scottish folk-music for me. Without her keen interest and enthusiasm, her advice on methodological matters and her knowledge and personal contacts in a field where I was still fumbling, I might have lost the essential contact with the living folk-music.

I also wish to thank Dr. Adina Forsgren, who guided me at the earliest stage of this work with her personal interest and scholarly knowledge; Dr. David Johnson, Edinburgh, and Professor Mary Ellen Lewis, Indiana University, who kindly took time to discuss with me some initial problems; Mr. William J. Bolton, Curator at the Burns Cottage Museum, Alloway, who supplied me with Burns documents and a study to work in; Dr. Lennart Kjellberg, who most generously offered to read the proofs and did so with several perceptive comments; Mrs. Agneta Ljunggren, who read the proofs and contributed invaluable stylistic emendations; Mr. Michael Srigley, who read the manuscript and suggested stylistic improvements; Mr. Hermann Wüscher, who gave useful editorial directions; Mr. Richard Glover, who kindly helped with some linguistic matters. Thanks are also due to the staff of the School of Scottish Studies for letting me listen to tape-recordings of Burns songs and Scottish folk-songs; to the Trustees of Burns Monument for giving me permission to quote from Burns's manuscript notes in his copies of *The Caledonian Pocket Companion, The Scots Musical Museum* and Ritson's *Select Collection of English Songs*; to Uppsala University and the Swedish Institute for generous grants which made it possible for me to persue my research in Burns's Caledonia; to the participants of Professor Sorelius's seminars, who took the trouble to read early chapters; to all my friends whose understanding, encouragements and support have been of great importance.

Last, but not least, I wish to thank my husband, Jan-Ingvar Roos, for his continuous interest and understanding. His own interest in Scottish culture and Scottish history has often been a source of inspiration. Henrik Roos, nine years old, must also be remembered here, for his patience when doors have been shut and silence has had to reign in the house.

References and Abbreviations

Kinsley   *The Poems and Songs of Robert Burns*. Ed. James Kinsley.
                3 vols. Oxford: Clarendon, 1968.
H-H   *The Poetry of Robert Burns*. Ed. William E. Henley and
                Thomas F. Henderson. 4 vols. Edinburgh: T. C. and E. C.
                Jack, 1901.
Dick, *The Songs* *The Songs of Robert Burns Now First Printed with the
                Melodies for Which They Were Written: A Study in Tone-
                Poetry*. Ed. James C. Dick. London: Henry Frowde, 1903.

The lyric texts are quoted from Kinsley and the songs are referred to by their
titles and numbers in his edition. Word explanations are given from the glossary in the same edition as are also biographical and historical facts concerning
the songs discussed. As references in my text to critical comments made by
Kinsley can be easily found in Vol. III under the number of the song, footnotes
or page-references are not given. Unless otherwise stated, italics in songs
quoted are always my own.

Other texts by Burns quoted and referred to in the body of the text:

1CPB   *Robert Burns's Commonplace Book 1783–1785*. Facsimile
                edition. Ed. James C. Ewing and Davidson Cook. Glasgow:
                Gowans and Gray, 1938.
Letter   *The Letters of Robert Burns*. Ed. J. De Lancey Ferguson. 2
                vols. Oxford: Clarendon, 1931. The serial number of the let-
                ter in this edition is given as a reference.
MMC   *The Merry Muses of Caledonia*. Ed. James Barke and Sid-
                ney Goodsir Smith. London: W. H. Allen, 1965.
Notes   *Notes on Scottish Song by Robert Burns: Written in an In-
                terleaved Copy of the Scots Musical Museum with Addi-
                tions by Robert Riddell and Others*. Ed. James C. Dick.
                London: Henry Frowde, 1908.

Musical examples are given from:

SMM   *The Scots Musical Museum Originally Published by James
                Johnson with Illustrations of the Lyric Poetry and Music of*

Scotland by William Stenhouse. Vol. I. 1853, facsimile ed., Hatboro, Pa.: Folklore Associates, 1962. My corrections of misprints in this edition as well as my additions of slurs are enclosed in square brackets.

Other abbreviations used in the text:

CPC   *The Caledonian Pocket Companion.* Ed. James Oswald. 12 vols. London, 1743—59 (dates approximate).

SC   *A Select Collection of Original Scotish Airs for the Voice.* Ed. George Thomson. 5 vols. London, 1793—1818.

Introduction

"Those who think that composing a Scotch song is a trifling business,
let them try."

Robert Burns, Letter 149

In 1793 Robert Burns wrote to George Thomson, one of the editors of his
songs,[1] and explained to him his method of composition: "I do not know the
air; & untill I am compleat master of a tune, in my own singing, (such as it is) I
never can compose for it." He makes it clear that the music was the incitement
to the poetry: he first considered the poetic sentiment corresponding to his idea
of the musical expression and then chose his theme (Letter 586). The music
thus decided the form and the rhythm of the lyric and it also suggested its expression. For a true appreciation and understanding of Burns's art, the lyric
texts should therefore always be analysed in conjunction with their respective
tunes and the songs be dealt with as unities of poetry and music.

The sense of unity in a song is attained when there is a mutual interaction
between its two elements, music and poetry, and when these are joined in such
a way that the music enlivens and enhances the poetry and the poetry par-
ticularizes the expression of the music. Such a union is not indissoluble, the
same tune may go equally well with another text or the same text have different
tunes. But the expression of the song will differ in different "combinations",
and the union of words and music may seem more or less organic. For a
successful wedding of text and tune it is therefore essential that the two
elements fit each other structurally and rhythmically, and that their general expressions are not too disparate. Archibald T. Davidson, in *Words and Music,*
has aptly expressed this conjunctive function of lyric and music in a song. He
says that a "text will supply meanings and a physical framework for the support of the music. Music, in its turn, will transfigure plain meanings and clothe
the verbal substance with a kind of incandescence that words by themselves
cannot achieve."[2]

Most songs of Burns arose from tune to text. The music gave birth to the
poetry and the poetry was begotten within the specific expression of the music.

[1] The term "song" in this study refers to the whole composition, consisting of both lyric and
tune.
[2] Archibald T. Davison, *Words and Music: A lecture delivered ... December 10, 1953*
(Washington: Library of Congress, 1954), p. 1.

1

Each stanza, each line and each word therefore often had a definite musical connotation for Burns by the time he got the lyric down on paper. Musical structure and rhythm limited his freedom as to form and poetic metre, and along with melody they guided his choice of theme. But structure, rhythm and melody were also potential instruments of a particular expression which could be used instead of words. The aim of the present study is to show how an essential part of the expression of the songs lies in their music as well as in the interaction between words and music, how a kind of synergism is created cooperatively by the lyric and the music, and how most songs suffer from being only read. The method has been to consider the two elements of the songs, the verbal and the musical, separately before analysing the whole text-tune complex. The form, rhythm and melody of the tune have been studied as well as their respective correspondences with the structure, metre and mood of the lyric.

Burns's indebtedness to music in the songs has been acknowledged by twentieth-century scholars, and they have realized that the poems should never be severed from their tunes.[3] But there are only scattered analyses of the songs *qua* songs, as entities composed of both lyric and tune, and no critic has yet made a systematic approach to a larger group of songs from the point of view of a textual-musical interrelationship. The most important critical works on Burns's songs take up the musical aspects in varying degrees. David Daiches discusses a few songs in a musical context, but the majority of those he submits to criticism are analysed from a more conventional point of view.[4] Christina Keith points out that the songs "have no objective reality of their own. They are projected by the tune. Fused into one with the music, they are like fire, struck from the tinder of the tune", but her analyses do not take the music into consideration.[5] In a long and important chapter on the songs, Thomas Crawford rightly points out that the "conflict of opinion over their worth arises partly from failure to consider them in a musical context".[6] He discusses the songs more thoroughly than any other critic and continuously reminds the reader of the dimension which the music adds to the lyric. However, as his book is meant to be a literary study, only a few songs are analysed from a strict poetical-musical point of view. The latest contribution to Burns scholarship has been

---

[3] For a critical article on scholarship on Burns's songs 1900–1950, see Robert D. Thornton, "Twentieth-Century Scholarship on the Songs of Robert Burns", *University of Colorado Studies: Series in Language and Literature,* No. 4 (Boulder, Col.: Univ. of Col. Press, 1953), pp. 75–92.

[4] David Daiches, *Robert Burns,* 2nd rev. ed. (London: André Deutsch, 1966).

[5] Christina Keith, *The Russet Coat: A Critical Study of Burns' Poetry and of Its Background* (London: Robert Hale, 1956), p. 125.

[6] Thomas Crawford, *Burns: A Study of the Poems and Songs* (Edinburgh: Oliver & Boyd, 1960), p. 261.

made by Cedric Thorpe Davie, who discusses the songs from the point of view of the musicologist.[7] He groups the songs according to the respective merits of the texts and the tunes, and the best songs are obviously the ones in which both lyric and music are good (there are also good lyrics matched to worthless tunes, poor words attached to beautiful tunes, and songs in which both text and tune are bad). Some of the songs of these four groups are briefly analysed, but then with more stress on the music than on the lyric.

Analyses of a few separate songs can also be found in shorter works. One of the earliest attempts to give due attention to the music of the songs was made by Alexander Keith in 1922. In his short book, *Burns and Folk-song,* he points out that "it is helpful to remember music's enhancement of verbal melody in studying Burns's songs or in arriving at a just appreciation of his lyrical genius",[8] and he also discusses some songs in relation to their tunes. In a short article Tom M. McCourt shows by analysing a few songs how important it is that the lyrics are sung to the tunes for which Burns originally wrote them.[9] Bertrand H. Bronson, who has thoroughly investigated the interrelation between music and poetry, especially in ballads and folk-songs, also discusses some of Burns's songs in his book *The Ballad as Song.* He does this from the point of view of the influence of simple tunes on the structural patterns of lyrical texts.[10] Robert D. Thornton is another Burns scholar who, in an anthology of the poems and songs, stresses the point that "severance of verses from music, particularly from the melody to which the song was composed, is inexcusably delusive for true appreciation".[11] He has, however, gone into only a very few of the songs with this aspect in mind.

Finally there will be mentioned the two editions of the songs which are most important from a musical point of view. James Dick did the pioneer work in 1903 in printing all the songs for the first time with their tunes. In his preface, and indeed in the very title of the collection, *The Songs of Robert Burns . . . A*

[7] Cedric Thorpe Davie, "Robert Burns, Writer of Songs", *Critical Essays on Robert Burns,* ed. Donald A. Low (London: Routledge, 1975), pp. 157—186.

[8] Alexander Keith, *Burns and Folk-song* (Aberdeen: D. Wyllie & Son, 1922), p. 14.

[9] Tom M. McCourt, "The Forgotten Songs of Robert Burns", *Étude Music Magazine,* 69 (1951), 12—13.

[10] Bertrand Harris Bronson, *The Ballad as Song* (Berkeley: Univ. of Calif. Press, 1969), pp. 306—11. See also short notes in his "Literature and Music", *Relations of Literary Study: Essays on Interdisciplinary Contributions,* ed. James Thorpe (New York: MLA, 1967), pp. 143—44, and in "Some Aspects of Music and Literature in the Eighteenth Century", in James E. Phillips and Bertrand H. Bronson, *Music & Literature in England in the Seventeenth and Eighteenth Centuries* (Los Angeles: William Andrews Clarke Memorial Library, 1953), pp. 51—54.

[11] *Robert Burns: Selected Poetry and Prose,* ed. Robert D. Thornton (Boston: Houghton Mifflin, 1966), p. v. See also his *The Tuneful Flame: Songs of Robert Burns as He Sang Them* (Kansas: Univ. of Kansas Press, 1957), Introd. Thornton also prints the tunes with his own arrangements.

Study in Tone-Poetry, he stresses the fact that these are *songs,* made to be sung and not read.[12] James Kinsley, the most recent in the line of Burns's editors, does not only print the tunes, but he also comments upon several songs from a textual-musical point of view.[13]

The present study is an attempt to fill the clear need for a more systematic textual-musical approach to a representative group of Burns's songs. As its scope does not allow for an investigation of all the songs, the choice has been limited to the ones printed in James Johnson's six volumes of *The Scots Musical Museum* (Edinburgh, 1787—1803). These songs form a group which is representative of Burns's art as a song-writer, and they are also considered by the critics as being his best. Dick points out that when working with Johnson, Burns "was entirely unfettered in his choice of airs and subjects, and his genius had free scope to revel in the kind of realistic human lyrics which had enthralled his countrymen for generations past".[14] Burns's collaboration with George Thomson, the editor of *A Select Collection of Original Scotish Airs for the Voice,* many times forced him into writing songs in a manner which was quite alien to him. The style of these songs is therefore often stilted, the themes are conventional, and the songs are also less successful as unities of music and poetry. From the large group of songs in *SMM* (about 200) I have excluded those which are mainly composed, or believed to be composed, of traditional lyric material.[15] I have also excluded the songs in which the tunes were attached to the lyrics after Burns had written them,[16] as well as those in which there is doubt as to the identity of the tune.[17] Burns's use of sources will be further discussed in Chapter 1, which also gives a short account of the biographical, social and musical background to Burns's song-writing.

To discuss Burns's songs from a musical-poetical angle will inevitably presuppose a basic knowledge of music on the reader's part, for indeed "the tone-deaf man" is "unfitted to judge Burns's songs", as Crawford bluntly puts it.[18] Musical discussions cannot be left out, nor can musical terminology be

---

[12] Dick, *The Songs,* pp. v—vii.

[13] Some of the analyses in this edition can also be found in James Kinsley, "The Music of the Heart", *Renaissance and Modern Studies,* 8 (1964), 44—50.

[14] Dick, *Notes,* p. xxxvi. See also Thorpe Davie, pp. 162, 174.

[15] Nos. 178, 185, 198—99, 201, 203, 205—06, 212, 216, 218, 240, 251, 284, 289—90, 294, 297—99, 304—08, 311, 314, 341—44, 349—54, 358—59, 366—68, 371, 374, 376—78, 381—82, 384, 407A, 453, 554, 556—58, 560—63, 565, 567—71, 573, 575, 577—78, 580—81, 584—89, 591—93, 596—99, 602—05 in Kinsley. The selection of songs is mainly based on Kinsley's comments, but collation has also been made with Dick, *The Songs* and H-H. References to the lyric sources of the songs will only be made if these sources are substantial parts of Burns's songs, or when it is of interest for the interpretation to know about them.

[16] Nos. 3, 66, 168, 217, 272, 316, 317 in Kinsley.

[17] Nos. 43, 65, 107, 181, 192, 226, 348, 461 in Kinsley.

[18] Crawford, p. 261.

4

avoided. As an introduction to the music of the songs, Chapter 2 will therefore explain the structure and idiom of folk-tunes in general and point out specific features of the Scottish ones.

But the present thesis is not musicological. The aim is to show the unity of poetry and music and the songs are analysed from both the musicologist's and the literary critic's point of view. Therefore, in Chapters 3—7, which deal with the songs themselves, the starting-point of the discussions are the literary themes, for in the themes both text and tune are embodied as well as the interaction between these two elements.[19]

---

[19] My grouping of the songs according to themes has to some extent been influenced by James Dick's nine groups in his edition of *The Songs,* as well as of Auguste Angellier's classification of the love songs; see his *Etude sur la vie et les œuvres de Robert Burns* (Paris: Librairie Hachette, 1892), Vol. II, pp. 235—313, and for an English extraction of the 25 categories, see Crawford, pp. 366—68. However, my restriction of the number of songs, and my consideration of the tunes as well as of the lyrics, have decided the final arrangement of my categories.

Chapter 1

The Background

In 1787 Burns met James Johnson, a devoted engraver who had embarked on the grand project of gathering and editing old Scottish songs for a one-volume collection called *The Scots Musical Museum*.[1] To become the assistant and co-editor of this work was for Burns not to start on a wholly new field but rather to take up the thread where he had left it earlier in life. Ever since he wrote his very first poem, "O once I lov'd" (1), he had had a latent passion for song-writing. In September 1785 he notes in his first *Commonplace Book:*

There is a degree of wild irregularity in many of the compositions & Fragments which are daily sung to them [the airs] by my compeers, the common people—a certain happy arrangement of old Scotch syllables, & yet, very frequently, nothing, not even *like* rhyme, or sameness of jingle at the ends of the lines.—This has made me sometimes imagine that perhaps, it might be possible for a Scotch Poet, with a nice, judicious ear, to set compositions to many of our most favorite airs, particularly that class of them mentioned above, independent of rhyme altogether. (*1CPB*, p. 38)

When he was fifteen he fell in love with a young girl and noticed that there was "some connection between Love, and Music & Poetry" (*1CPB*, p. 3) and he "committed the sin of RHYME" by "giving an embodied vehicle in rhyme" to "her favorite reel" (Letter 125). After that first attempt at fitting words to music he would find his inspiration in the songs and tunes of Scotland. Not until he met James Johnson, however, did he get the incitement to get really engrossed in song-writing. His antiquarian interest was passionate. He "begg'd, borrow'd" and stole all the songs he came across (Letter 193) and made "pilgrimages" to the places where the songs had originated (Letter 535).

---

[1] I am indebted to the following books on the life on Robert Burns for the biographical facts in this chapter: J. De Lancey Ferguson, *Pride and Passion: Robert Burns 1759–1796* (New York: OUP, 1939); Robert T. Fitzhugh, *Robert Burns: The Man and the Poet. A Round Unvarnished Account* (Boston: Houghton Mifflin, 1970); Hans Hecht, *Robert Burns: The Man and His Work,* trans. Jane Lymburn, 2nd rev. ed. (Edinburgh: William Hodge, 1950); Frank Bliss Snyder, *The Life of Robert Burns* (New York: Macmillan, 1932). For more extensive accounts of the revival of Scottish song, see Henry George Farmer, *A History of Music in Scotland* (London: Hinrichsen, 1947), pp. 249–61; David Johnson, *Music and Society in Lowland Scotland in the Eighteenth Century* (London: OUP, 1972), Ch. vii; Francis Collinson, *The Traditional and National Music of Scotland* (1966; rpt. London: Routledge, 1970), pp. 120–32. The Italian influence during this period has been dealt with by Ronald D. Jack, *The Italian Influence on Scottish Literature* (Edinburgh: Edinburgh UP, 1972), Ch. v.

The last nine years of his short life (he was thirty-seven when he died) were devoted almost exclusively to song-writing, song-collecting and song-editing. He grew extremely knowledgeable on the subject and said himself that he had "paid more attention to every description of Scots songs than perhaps any body living" had done before him (*Notes,* p. 5). With so much enthusiasm and so much energy did he go into this project that after some time he had become the virtual editor of *SMM.* The first volume was almost ready when Burns met Johnson, but the following ones have the clear mark of his hand. Johnson was not really competent for the task he had undertaken, but thanks to Burns the collection grew into as many as six volumes, each covering one hundred songs. When the fifth was ready for the press the poet died and it took Johnson seven years to compile the sixth and last volume on his own, although he had material enough, material which Burns had collected for him earlier.

Burns also wrote songs for George Thomson's *A Select Collection of Original Scotish Airs for the Voice,* but the understanding between these two men was not as close as that between Johnson and Burns. Thomson's object was not to preserve Scots songs, but to purify them of the Scottish language, to accommodate the verses to the taste of his genteel readers, to refine their style and to harmonize the tunes so that they would be better fit for concerts. For this purpose he engaged composers like Haydn, Pleyel, and Beethoven to write piano accompaniments. He wanted Burns to write standard English poems in a genteel style, he suggested a lot of changes to "improve" them, and he chose the tunes at his own whim, completely disregarding the instructions which Burns gave him. The collaboration forced Burns into defending and explaining his aesthetic intentions and his poetical-musical ideas in a copious correspondence, which is very illuminating as to his theories of song-writing and on his creative process.

With Johnson Burns had a free hand to carry out his ideas, whereas with Thomson he was pushed and pressed all the time into composing songs in a style which was quite alien to him and with which he did not feel at his ease. He found that to the "simple pathos, or rustic sprightliness" of Scots music the "slight intermixture of Scots words & phraseology" was better suited "than any English verses whatever" (Letter 535) and he complains to Thomson: "These English Songs gravel me to death.—I have not that command of the language that I have of my native tongue.—In fact, I think my ideas are more barren in English than in Scotish" (Letter 644). It should be pointed out in this context, however, that his failure with the English songs was not in any way due to linguistic difficulties, but to the fact that he then attempted a style and manner of writing with which he had nothing in common.[2]

---

[2] Frank Bliss Snyder, *Robert Burns: His Personality, His Reputation and His Art* (Toronto: The Univ. of Toronto Press, 1936), p. 96.

In Burns's production there is also a small number of songs which were printed without tunes in the first editions of his poems[3] and a group of songs which were never printed at all during his life-time. To this group belong *The Jolly Beggars* ("Love and Liberty—a Cantata", 184), eight songs connected through recitatives, and *The Merry Muses of Caledonia,* Burns's private collection of bawdy songs.

Burns grew up in a society which was steeped in song and he was used to hearing people around him sing. His mother, his mother's maid, who had "the largest collection in the county of tales and songs" (Letter 125), and many others accustomed his ear to the Scottish songs. These songs he stored in his memory to use them later in life. Although he was also indebted to English verse-making through the books which his tutor, John Murdoch, provided him with, it was with the folk-literature and to a certain extent with the poems by the Scottish poets Ramsay and Ferguson that he could identify himself. His education came mainly from the common people and from life and not from books.

In Edinburgh he would also meet with a lively society of music-makers, but of a different sort. In the 1780's there was a curious blend of folk and classical music in this city. What Burns heard here, as opposed to what he had been used to in the countryside, was not music of the genuine, untarnished folk-tradition. Recitals of Scottish songs were given in private circles as well as in St. Cecilia's Hall, the concert hall of Edinburgh. Italian singers came to delight the audience of St. Cecilia's Hall, not only with the standard concert repertoire, but also with their renderings of Scottish songs. According to Henry Mackenzie, one of these singers, Tenducci, sang them in a "style suited to that tenderness and simplicity which are the characteristics of the ancient Scottish air, without any of those graces of ornaments which are foreign to them".[4] Yet this singer was an exception. The simplicity of style in folk-songs was bound to be influenced by the classical and Italian ideals, and David Johnson, who has made a fine analysis of folk and classical music in eighteenth-century Scotland, points out that ". . . Foreign singers decorated the tunes mercilessly in order to squeeze the last drop of sentiment out of them, and tempi were progressively slowed down until 'Scots songs' were nearly always slow songs."[5]

The revival of Scottish song got its real start in 1723, when Allan Ramsay published the first volume of his *Tea-table Miscellany: A Collection of Choice Songs* (printed in Edinburgh), an anthology of songs either restored from old

[3] Robert Burns, *Poems, Chiefly in the Scottish Dialect* (Kilmarnock: John Wilson, 1786); *Poems, Chiefly in the Scottish Dialect* (Edinburgh: William Creech, 1787); *Poems, Chiefly in the Scottish Dialect,* 2nd enl. ed., 2 vols. (Edinburgh: William Creech, 1793).

[4] Henry Mackenzie, *The Anecdotes and Egotisms* (Oxford: OUP, 1927), p. 76.

[5] Johnson, *Music and Society,* p. 144.

8

ones, or written by unknown authors or by himself, and all to be sung to traditional tunes. However, Ramsay did not realize the importance of actually printing the tunes as well, and so thirty-eight of his songs were "stolen" and brought into William Thomson's *Orpheus Caledonius,* printed in London in 1725. This was the first collection of songs to be printed with their respective tunes, and it was to be followed by many other collections of songs, with and without tunes.[6] But also these collections, although they drew on traditional material, reflect the blend of the folk- and art-styles. The title of Ramsay's book implies that it was meant to be used by the upper-class ladies by the tea-table, and as David Johnson points out, it was common among the Edinburgh upper-class ladies to sing folk-songs and traditional ballads after supper.[7] William Montgomerie shows that much of the genuine folk-poetry in these collections (and also in some of Burns's songs) was spoiled by being "improved", and by being under the strong influence of eighteenth-century English genteel poetry.[8] James Bruce Duncan, the folk-song collector, expresses the same opinion and maintains that the folk-songs have "suffered from the contact of the literary song proceeding from Allan Ramsay, Burns, Baroness Nairne, Hogg, Tannahill, and the great horde of other imitators".[9]

As a result of the growing popularity of dancing there was also an abundance of instrumental collections. The fiddle had superseded the bagpipe as the principal dance instrument and there was consequently a sudden need for fiddle-music. The traditional tunes were of course profusely represented, but as these did not suffice to supply the need, also a large number of new ones were written in what was believed to be the old Scottish style. These collections, with their variations for the fiddle or the flute in a more or less classical style, mirror yet another aspect of the mixture of the folk- and art-traditions.

It was this vogue for Scottish song which kindled Burns's muse and he quickly made himself familiar with all the printed songs and tunes of Scotland. His knowledge was extensive: "I was so lucky lately as to pick up an entire copy of Oswald's Scots music, and I think I shall make glorious work out of it. I want much Anderson's Collection of strathspeys &c., and then I think I will have all the music of the country", he says in a letter to Johnson (Letter 452). In a letter to Thomson he asks for "a list of your airs, with the first line of the verses", emphasizing that the first lines will suffice, for he will either be familiar

---

[6] Dick gives an extensive bibliographic list of songs printed without music, songs printed with music, as well as of instrumental music; see Dick, *The Songs,* pp. xxviii–xliii.

[7] Johnson, *Music and Society,* p. 17.

[8] William Montgomerie, "Folk Poetry and Robert Burns", *Burns Chronicle and Club Directory,* 2nd ser., 12 (1950), 27–28.

[9] P. N. Shuldham-Shaw and E. B. Lyle, ed., "Folk-Song in the North-East: J. B. Duncan's Lecture, 1908", *Scottish Studies,* 18 (1974), 8.

with the song or know in which collection to find it (Letter 507).[10] Since there were no more than about two hundred songs actually printed with the music, the main sources for his tunes would be the collections of instrumental dance tunes.[11] His own copy of the largest of them, James Oswald's *Caledonian Pocket Companion* (which he refers to as "Oswald's Scots music" in the letter to Johnson) has many of his own annotations which show that he had studied many of the tunes in great detail (see below, n. 17). His many references to this collection and others, his letters, his annotations in the interleaved copy of *SMM* (Vols. I–IV) and in the Laing manuscripts,[12] and his notes in Ritson's *A Select Collection of English Songs*[13] also show that he had a considerable and extensive knowledge of both songs and tunes. When he met with songs which had not been printed before, he had them noted down from *viva voce* and thereby prevented many of them from falling into oblivion.

The blend of the folk- and art-traditions in eighteenth-century Scotland is reflected also in Burns's song-production. Burns occupies an interesting intermediate position between these two styles, and his achievement was, as Kinsley puts it, "the transmutation of folk-song into art-song".[14] Typical of folk-song is the oral transmission and the continuous recreation. People forget the words or the tunes and reshape the songs according to their own tastes and needs or in order to make them representative of their culture and its characteristics. As a result of this the composer is often (but not always) forgotten. Folk-song is also functional, it is unprofessional and it has a strong link with the past.[15] According to this definition of folk-song, although very broad, Burns's songs undoubtedly belong to the genus art-song. They

[10] For an article on old song books owned or known by Burns, see Davidson Cook, "Burns and old song books", *The Scottish Musical Magazine,* 3, Nos. 8 and 11 (1927), 147–49, 207–09.

[11] Dick, *The Songs,* p. xiii.

[12] Printed by Davidson Cook as "Annotations of Scottish Songs by Burns: An Essential Supplement to Cromek and Dick", *Annual Burns Chronicle and Club Directory,* 31 (1922), 1–21. The annotations in the interleaved copy of *SMM* are printed in Dick's *Notes.*

[13] Joseph Ritson, ed., *A Select Collection of English Songs,* 3 vols. (London, 1783). Burns's copies of the collection contain his comments on several songs, most of them being of the type "Set also by . . .", "Better set by . . .", "Not so well set".

[14] Kinsley, "The Music of the Heart", p. 52.

[15] This definition can only be a generalization, but for the purpose of the present study it is not necessary to go into further details. For more extensive definitions and discussions on the nature of folk-song, see Bruno Nettl, *Folk and Traditional Music of the Western Continents* (Englewood Cliffs, N.J.: Prentice-Hall, 1965), Ch. i; Maud Karpeles, *An Introduction to English Folk Song* (London: OUP, 1973), Chs. i–ii; Cecil J. Sharp, *English Folk Song: Some Conclusions,* 4th ed., rev. Maud Karpeles, 1965; rpt. (London: EP Publishing Ltd., 1972), Chs. i–iv; Johnson, *Music and Society,* Ch. i. For a discussion of the dichotomy between folk-song and art-song, see Thomas Crawford, "Scottish Popular Ballads and Lyrics of the Eighteenth and Early Nineteenth Centuries: Some Preliminary Conclusions", *Studies in Scottish Literature,* 1 (1963), 49–63.

were written for the specific purpose of being printed, and when Burns studied the tunes from a printed source or when he listened to them, when he tried to find the right sentiment and words to fit these tunes, he was to a high degree the individual craftsman. Yet there are elements in many of his songs which make it impossible to conceive of them exclusively as art-songs. The themes and the style of these songs with their simplicity, their refrains, their choruses and their repetitive patterns are traditional, and a large number of the songs contain fragments of old material or take their start from a traditional stanza or chorus. But there are also songs whose style is English, neo-classic and somewhat artificial, and these have of course nothing in common with the folk-songs. The same is true of the songs written for tunes which were not traditional in style but written by contemporary composers like James Oswald and Robert Riddell.

But it must be remembered that Burns worked within a living tradition. Although he found much lyric and musical material in printed collections, and although he was also influenced by the eighteenth-century neo-classic style, his song-writing was founded on what he heard. His attitude to George Thomson is symptomatic, for he strongly objected when the latter let composers like Haydn or Pleyel meddle with the simple and unpretentious style of the tunes: "whatever Mr Pleyel does, let him not alter one iota of the original Scots Air ... But, let our National Music preserve its native features" (Letter 559). He was not trying to achieve anything new, but rather do what the Scots folk had done before him without his own contribution being noticed too much. Therefore, he was very unwilling to acknowledge his authorship in *SMM,* and as he felt that he was only the transmitter, rather than the creator of the songs, he also refused to accept money for them.

What we know about Burns's knowledge of music has been somewhat obscured by his own humble attitude. To George Thomson he says: "Of the Poetry, I speak with confidence; but the Music is a business where I hint my ideas with the utmost diffidence" (Letter 587). It is, however, obvious that his knowledge was quite considerable, although he was "untaught & untutored by Art" (Letter 582). He expresses himself with the greatest assurance on minute technical matters in the letters to Thomson, he has a fine sense of the latent expressions of various tunes, and he is well versed in what is the traditional style and peculiar features of Scottish songs. The few surviving musical manuscripts[16] reveal that he had a basic knowledge of musical notation, as do

---

[16] The only musical MS of a whole song that is extant is that of "Here's his health in water" (583 A, Hastie MS, f. 128, see ill.). But there are also short musical examples in a letter to Thomson (two bars of "O saw ye bonie Lesley", 339, Letter 515) and on the MS for "Ca' the ewes" (185, Hastie MS, f. 56). The Hastie MSS (Add. MSS 22307) are kept at the British Library and consist of material for *SMM* (171 songs, some letters, and instructions to Johnson).

also the corrections of misprints in his copies of *CPC* and *SMM* and the remarks on key and tempo in *CPC*.[17] His notes in *CPC* also shed light upon his opinion about the tunes as he makes remarks like "fine", "bon", "pretty", and "beautiful" on some of them, others he singles out by marking them with a cross.[18]

Burns could also play the fiddle a little, but he mostly left the execution of the quick dance-tunes to the better fiddlers. He had once tried his hand at the German flute, and at Lochlea and Mossgiel he attended singing-classes for a few months. His singing, however, was not very good, although he could hum the tunes for himself. Therefore, when working on the songs, women like Jean Armour, his wife, Kirsty Flint, his neighbour at Ellisland, and the young Janet Cruickshank, the daughter of a friend of his, used to help him by singing them over and over again. In public Burns himself preferred to recite his poems rather than sing his songs. Dr. James McKittrick Adair gives this account of the Stirlingshire tour: "Many songs were sung; which I mention for the sake of observing, that then when Burns was called on in his turn, he was accustomed, instead of singing, to recite one or other of his own shorter poems, with a tone and emphasis, which though not correct or harmonious, were impressive and pathetic."[19] It is not known to what extent Burns was able to take down notes from *viva voce*. He might have "evolved some kind of musical shorthand", as one of his critics calls it,[20] to use when he could not rely upon anybody else, but

[17] As these annotations and corrections of misprints have not been mentioned in a critical work on Burns before (they are overlooked by Davidson Cook in his article on Burns's copy of *CPC*, see below, n. 18), and as they throw some light on his musical abilities, they will be noted here. In Book IV, p. 30 ("The Maid's Complaint") the four semi-quavers in the 10th bar have correctly been changed to quavers, and in Book VIII, p. 15 ("Pangs of Love") Burns has added two crotchets to the dotted minim in the 16th bar to indicate another way of ending the song. Similarly, in Book III of the interleaved copy of *SMM* he has corrected a crotchet to a quaver in song 232, p. 241 ("The Lazy mist"), and in his copy of *SMM*, Vol. II, there are similar corrections, as Frank B. Snyder has pointed out (*The Life of Robert Burns*, p. 414). This, of course, does not mean that Burns went through the collections in order to find misprints (there are some which he has not noticed), but it shows that he was meticulous enough to correct them when he found them, and that he had the elementary knowledge of musical notation necessary to notice them at all. The comments on the key of two tunes in *CPC* are puzzling: in Book I, p. 31 ("Peggy I must love thee"), Burns has written "in A" although the song is printed in G, and in Book V, p. 12 ("The Shepherds of Yarrow"), he has written "I think in G" although the song is in a modal key with A as the tonal centre. This could mean that Burns wanted the tune to be transposed, or it could simply indicate a lack of musical knowledge in this respect. In Book VIII, p. 9 ("The Widow's Lilt") there is an example of Burns's habit of slowing down tempi to bring out new expressions (see below, Ch. 2, ii): Burns's note here says "in D slow", although the tempo is marked as "brisk".

[18] These annotations are recorded by Davidson Cook in his article "Burns's 'Oswald': The 'Caledonian Pocket Companion' ", *The Scots Magazine*, 19, No. 5 (1933), 379—81.

[19] *Robert Burns's Tours of the Highlands and Stirlingshire 1787*, ed. Raymond Lamont Brown (Ipswich: The Boydell Press, 1973), p. 52.

[20] Catherine Carswell, *The Life of Robert Burns* (London: Chatto & Windus, 1930), pp. 274—75, n. 1.

to judge from his letters, it seems that he mostly had others to help him, e.g. Stephen Clarke, the musical editor of *SMM*. As far as book knowledge is concerned Burns had read James Beattie's aesthetic essay on the union of poetry and music,[21] William Tytler's, as he calls it, "amusing history of Scots music" (*Notes*, p. 3),[22] as well as John Aikin's *Essay on Song-Writing,* in which there is a discussion on the nature of songs and song-writing.[23]

Burns's contributions to *SMM* were marked either by R, B or X, standing for his own pieces (Letter 280), or by Z, standing for songs "given to the world as old verses to their respective tunes" (Letter 285). Unfortunately, these markings have not proved very trustworthy, for in the same letter Burns admits that in "a good many of them [the songs], little more than the Chorus is ancient; tho' there is no reason for telling every body this piece of intelligence" (Letter 285). From other sources, too, such as other letters, the interleaved copy of *SMM* and the Law manuscript (a "List of Songs for 3rd Volume of the *Scots Musical Museum*", compiled by Burns and sent to Johnson) we know that several unmarked songs were written by Burns. On the other hand, there are songs which Johnson ascribed to Burns in *SMM* ("Written by Mr. Burns") but which later scholars have proved to be based on traditional material in various degrees. There is thus no unambiguous evidence of Burns's authorship in many of the songs.

Thomas Crawford has classified Burns's songs according to their amount of traditional material.[24] As the first group he mentions the songs which were old and went into *SMM* untouched by Burns's hand. Others (the second group) Burns tried to improve by changing the traditional text here and there, and these are the ones where it has proved extremely difficult to establish what is traditional and what is actually by Burns. The third group consists of songs of which Burns only knew an old chorus or a line or two. From these fragments he created a new poem. The fourth group consists of songs "which are predominantly mosaics of traditional phrases set to old tunes" and the fifth, finally, is the large group of songs written wholly by Burns. Altogether Burns contributed about 200 songs to *SMM*. It should be pointed out here that the traditional material was not only orally collected by Burns; he also found many old fragments and suggestions in printed sources and then particularly in

---

[21] James Beattie, "On Poetry and Music, as they affect the Mind", *Essays* (Edinburgh: William Creech, 1776), pp. 347—580.
[22] William Tytler, "A Dissertation on the Scottish Music", in Hugo Arnot, *The History of Edinburgh from the Earliest Accounts to the Present Time* (Edinburgh, 1779).
[23] John Aikin, *Essays on Song-Writing,* 2nd ed. (Warrington: William Eyres, 1774). This is the edition which Burns had read, see Davidson Cook, "Burns and old song books", p. 149.
[24] Crawford, pp. 267—68.

David Herd's collection *The Ancient and Modern Scots Songs* and possibly also in the latter's manuscripts.[25]

In most cases Burns indicated clearly in his manuscripts which tunes he intended for his poems. In *SMM* the songs were rightly printed with these tunes, unless they had been used before in the same collection for other texts. In these few cases Johnson preferred to have a new tune for Burns's song. In *SC*, on the other hand, many poems were coupled to tunes which were not at all authorized by Burns. Thorpe Davie points out that "whereas in *SMM* only 9 songs are printed with music differing from that which the poet had in mind when writing them, the total of such tunes, mostly unauthorized, in Thomson is not less than 43, and almost certainly is more".[26]

The question must be put whether the versions of the tunes printed in *SMM* agree with Burns's intentions, or if there is a discrepancy between his conception of the tunes, the way he was humming them to himself, or the way he had heard them and worked with them, and the final printed versions. The man who was responsible for these versions was Stephen Clarke, the musical editor of *SMM*, who not only harmonized the tunes, that is, provided them with a figured bass, but also arranged them.[27] What was the nature of his arrangements, to what extent did he change Burns's musical manuscripts, the transcriptions made of orally collected tunes, or the printed versions to which Burns often referred him and Johnson, and last but not least, were these changes in accordance with Burns's own intentions? The answer can only be conjectural as so much valuable material has been lost. The fact is that Clarke was rather indolent, irrecoverable tunes were lost through his negligence, and Burns complains in a letter that it was Clarke's usual habit to cast the songs sent to him "*at the cocks*" (Letter 616). It may be guessed that not only songs but also letters and musical manuscripts disappeared in this way.

Some conclusions can be drawn from the material we have, however. Burns had clear and definite ideas which he put through to Johnson and Clarke, partly in his letters and in the form of instructions on the manuscripts, partly, it may be guessed, at the "frequent meetings & consultations" (Letter 348) which

[25] David Herd, ed., *The Ancient and Modern Scots Songs, heroic ballads, &c. now first collected into one body,* 2nd enl. ed., 2 vols. (Edinburgh, 1776). This is the edition which Burns most probably used, see Cook, "Burns and old song books", p. 149. The manuscripts are printed by Hans Hecht in *Songs from David Herd's Manuscripts* (Edinburgh: William J. Hay, 1904). Crawford points out that, although it looks like it, Burns did not necessarily always take his material from Herd; he might simply have tapped the same living source; see Crawford, p. 277, n. 60. For a discussion on Herd and Burns, see Hecht, *Robert Burns,* pp. 198—201 and *Songs from David Herd's Manuscripts,* p. 51.

[26] Thorpe Davie, p. 164.

[27] Very little is known about Stephen Clarke, but a good account of him is given in David Fraser Harris, *Saint Cecilia's Hall* (Edinburgh: Oliphant Anderson and Ferrier, 1911), pp. 100—06.

14

he had with Clarke. This was during his time in Edinburgh, but also in Dumfries, where Clarke visited him. His musical directions are mainly concerned with the organization of the lyric to the tune (for example the problems of which stanza goes with which part of the tune or whether the high or low part of it takes the chorus), and I have found that with a few exceptions these directions were followed.

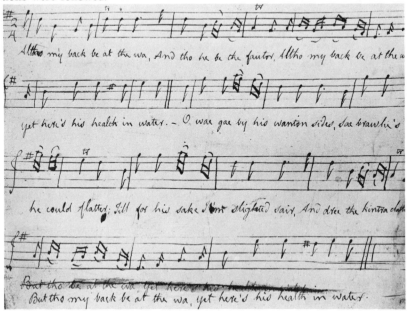

Burns's musical manuscript of "Here's his health in water" (583 A, Hastie MS, f. 128). Reproduced by permission of the British Library Board.

In the cases where the tunes had been printed before, Burns often told Johnson in which collection or collections he could find them. For "John come kiss me now" (343), for example, he gives the following instruction: "You will find this tune in McGibbon's, & and many other collections" (Hastie MS, f. 62). Very often, however, these tunes, especially the fiddle ones, which were heavily edited with ornamentations and variations, did not fit Burns's poems exactly. They had to be simplified and the note-value and rhythm accommodated to the number of syllables and to the poetical rhythm. At this point Clarke comes in, for the necessary rhythmic adjustments and arrangements were made by him. But a comparison which I have made between the versions of the tunes suggested by Burns and the ones finally printed in *SMM* shows that only very small rhythmic and sometimes melodic changes have been made. References in letters and manuscripts suggest that Burns sent in more musical manuscripts than the ones which are extant (see n. 16). It is to be doubted, however, that even these were printed exactly as Burns had noted them. A comparison between the only extant manuscript of a whole song and its printed version shows that the latter diverges in rhythmic details from Burns's own manuscript.[28]

It seems then that Clarke's musical arrangements mainly consisted of rhythmic and slight melodic adjustments of the tunes to the lyric texts. As Burns seldom gave instructions about such matters, and as he often left it open to Clarke to choose the best version of a particular tune, we may guess that he accepted the latter's adjustments and that they agreed with his idea of the expression of the song. What was discussed during Clarke's and Burns's meetings we shall never know, but to judge from the letters it seems that the cooperation was of the most fruitful kind. Burns had a very high opinion of Clarke and he often took his advice:

Our friend, Clarke, than whom, you know, there is not a better judge of the subject, complains that in the air "Lee-rig," the accent is to be altered. (Letter 559)

For instance, I am just now making verses for Rothemurche's Rant, an air which puts me in raptures: & in fact, unless I be pleased with the tune, I never can make verses to it. Here I have Clarke on my side, who is a judge that I will pit against any of you.—Rothemurche, he says, is an air both original & beautiful; & on his recommendation I have taken the first part of the tune for a chorus, & the fourth or last part for the song. (Letter 637)

Furthermore, as Burns became the unofficial editor-in-chief of *SMM*, and as he proof-read many of the songs, he had plenty of opportunity to object when he had reason to. Such is the case with "Craigieburn-wood—A Song" (340), and in a letter to Johnson Burns complains: "I received your letter with the proofs of two songs, but Mr Clarke has mistaken one of them, the song 'Craigieburnwood,' sadly, having put the chorus to the wrong part of the

---

[28] The tune of "Here's his health in water" is also to be found in *A Selection of Scotch, English, Irish, and Foreign Airs*, ed. James Aird (Glasgow, 1788), III, No. 401, a collection which Burns refers to many times in his instructions. I have compared Burns's MS (see ill.) and the Aird-version, and this comparison shows that the MS is clearly a copy of the printed air. The key is the same and the trills are placed above the same notes. There is only a slight difference in the rhythm, Aird having fewer dotted quavers than Burns. But why should Burns want to copy a tune from a collection which Johnson most certainly possessed himself? Why does he refer Johnson to Aird for several other songs, but not for this one? The reason might have been that he wanted to indicate that dotted rhythm went better with the poetical rhythm; the dots in Burns's version all fall at the end of a poetical line (i.e. bars 2, 4 and 6), thereby marking it off from the beginning of the next line. When, however, the MS got into the hands of Clarke the air underwent further changes. In the printed version (*SMM* No. 480) some dotted quavers have been changed back to undotted ones (bars 6, 14, 18), the semi-quaver figure in bar 5 has been dispensed with in favour of one note for each syllable and there are also a few other minor differences. Finally, the tempo of the song has been changed on the way, from "Andantino" in Aird, not marked at all in the MS, to "Lively" in *SMM*.—This throws some light on Burns's way of working with an air and it suggests that Stephen Clarke had a hand in the arrangements not only of instrumental tunes already printed, but also of Burns's own musical MSS.

tune—so I have given it to him to correct" (Letter 452). Also the correspondence with George Thomson shows that Burns did object when his ideas were not met with understanding. Therefore, on the basis of the evidence we have, we may take it that the tunes of the songs in *SMM* on the whole agree with Burns's musical-poetical ideas and intentions.

Before proceeding to a discussion of the songs themselves, there will be an introduction to their music in the following chapter. As my method when studying the tunes has been to examine form, rhythm and melody, these three aspects will be dealt with one by one, and the terminology and methodological tools of the musical discussions will be explained.

Chapter 2

The Music

i. Form

Scottish folk-songs, like most European folk-songs, are strophic.[1] The poems consist of stanzas with repeated rhyme-patterns, and the tunes are most commonly built up of four phrases (two-bar phrases or four-bar phrases) which correspond to the four, or four plus four, lines of the stanza. Each four-bar phrase is conventionally designated by a capital letter, and each two-bar phrase by a small letter (example 1). One of these phrases is often repeated and the form of the tune may then be e.g. AABA or ABCB when long (four four-bar phrases) or e.g. aabc or abab when short (four two-bar phrases). A variation of a section is commonly marked by a superscript number, e.g. A^1 is a variation of A, and the bar-number of a section by a figure below the letter, e.g. B_3 is bar 3 of B. The second and fourth phrases, or bars, end on a cadence, the middle-cadence (MC) and the end-cadence (EC), where the latter normally resolves on the tonic (the first note of the scale). The cadence can be compared to the full-stop in language; it serves the same function of terminating phrases, of bringing to a rest or marking the division between connected phrases (example 1). On these cadences the rhymes of the poem conveniently fall, abcb (example 2), but the rhyme-pattern can also be e.g. abab, aaba, or aaab. If the cadence is a long note or a note followed by a rest, the effected pattern of stressed syllables in the stanza will become 4-3-4-3 (example 2). This is the so-called "ballad metre", which is not only restricted to ballads but is used in all kinds of folk-songs. When there is no held cadence, the metre will become 4-4-4-4 (example 3).

The traditional tunes have a two-part structure, where the second of the two sections in most cases lies higher, usually a fifth higher (example 1). Often the

[1] I am indebted to the following authors for my account of the music of folk-songs: Bronson, *The Ballad as Song*, Chs. iii, v, vii, ix; Collinson, Ch. i; George S. Emmerson, *Rantin' Pipe and Tremblin' String: A History of Scottish Dance Music* (London: J. M. Dent, 1971), Chs. vii, ix; J. W. Hendren, *A Study of Ballad Rhythm: With Special Reference to Ballad Music*, Princeton Studies in English, No. 14 (Princeton: Princeton UP, 1936); Karpeles, Chs. iii, iv; Nettl, *Folk and Traditional Music of the Western Continents*, Chs. ii-iv; Sharp, Chs. v—vii. For the methodological approach to the music of the songs I am partly indebted to Bruno Nettl, *Theory and Method in Ethnomusicology* (London: The Free Press of Glencoe, 1964), Ch. v.

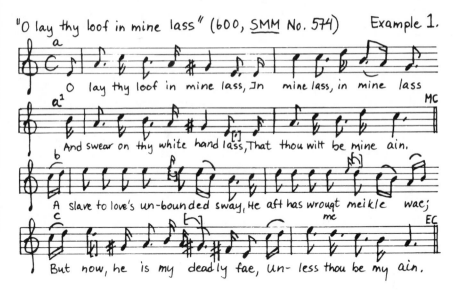

"O lay thy loof in mine lass" (600, SMM No. 574)   Example 1.

a

O lay thy loof in mine lass, In mine lass, in mine lass

a¹   MC

And swear on thy white hand lass, That thou wilt be mine ain.

b

A slave to love's un-boun-ded sway, He aft has wrougt mei-kle wae;

c   EC

But now, he is my dead-ly fae, Un- less thou be my ain.

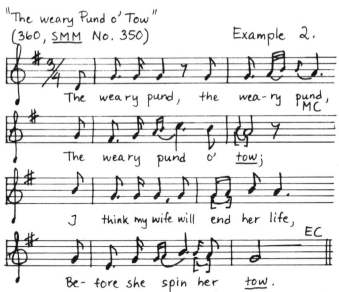

"The weary Pund o' Tow"
(360, SMM No. 350)   Example 2.

The weary pund, the wea-ry pund,
                                MC

The weary pund o' tow;

I think my wife will end her life,
                              EC

Be- fore she spin her tow.

last (or last two) bars of the first and second halves of the tune are identical and these "tags" may then carry a refrain. Repetitions in a lyric, which may seem so unimaginative on the printed page undergo an important transformation when wedded to a tune. Music can tolerate far more repetitions than poetry can, and its emotive import is often intensified by the repetition of a theme. It takes on a "new significance by being repeated, like an image under a succession of varicolored lenses", as Bronson puts it.[2] This effect is planted on to the lyric and repeated lines for repeated musical phrases may therefore be subtly and expressively varied. If repeated lines are set to different musical phrases, the change of expression between the two will be even more marked.

Much of the structural interdependence of text and tune is of an elementary kind common to all song-writing. It is obvious that the tune sets the form of the stanza and decides its rhythm. Phrase-endings, the cadences, usually correspond to the completion of a thought, one-syllable words, such as "O" and "Man" at the end of a line are there to accomodate the rhythm, and the rhyme-patterns, refrains and repetitions of traditional folk-songs are no doubt often suggested by the pattern of the musical phrases. Burns's achievement is founded on the folk-song tradition and it is only natural that what is typical of that tradition will also be found in his songs. But his art rises above a merely mechanical interdependence of lyric and music, for he takes advantage of the structure of the tune and makes it correspond to the sentiment of the lyric, or he gives the structure a significance of its own in the total expression of the song.

ii. Rhythm

Rhythm is the common element of both music and poetry, and rhythm is the pillar on which both arts rest. Without a rhythmic structure poetry falls into prose and without rhythm there is no music; it "is a *sine qua non* of the art" as Cooper and Meyer define it.[3] In songs words adapt to the time-value of the notes. They are prolonged or abbreviated, and the theories of poetic metre are not applicable to a discussion of poetry which is written for music and meant to be sung. They have to be replaced by those of musical rhythm and as Jack M. Stein points out, musical notes are almost always of longer duration than the syllables of words. Therefore any song will last longer than the poem alone.[4] But there is also a certain influence of words on musical rhythm and an awareness of the poetic metre also when the songs are sung. As an example of such a rhythmic interplay between text and tune the chorus of "Song.—Composed at Auchtertyre on Miss Euphemia Murray of Lentrose" (179) can be mentioned. In *SMM* (No. 180) the first and third lines of this chorus are set to exactly the same melodic phrases. However, the rhythm differs between the

[2] Bronson, "Literature and Music", p. 129; see also Calvin S. Brown, *Music and Literature: A Comparison of the Arts* (1948; rpt. Athens, Georgia: The Univ. of Georgia Press, 1949), p. 47.

[3] Grosvenor W. Cooper and Leonard B. Meyer, *The Rhythmic Structure of Music* (Chicago: The Univ. of Chicago Press, 1960), p. v.

[4] Jack M. Stein, *Poem and Music in the German Lied from Gluck to Hugo Wolf* (Cambridge, Mass.: Harvard UP, 1971), p. 13.

two, as it has been adjusted to the speech-rhythm of the lyric. In the first line ("Blythe, blythe, and *merry* was she") there is a snap (see below, p. 24) for "merry", as the first syllable of that word is short and strongly accented. In the third, on the other hand ("Blythe by the *banks of* Ern"), the same note is dotted in order to suit the long vowel of "banks" (example 3).

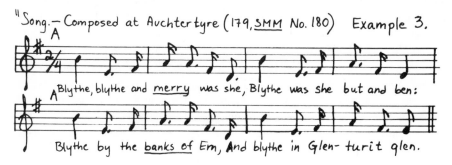

Rhythmic tension is created by an alternation of strong and weak beats. The rhythmic pattern can be duple (the beats are grouped in two, e.g. 2/4 time), triple (a group of three beats, e.g. 3/4-time) or quadruple, which is really double duple time (four beats, e.g. 4/4-time). There is also compound time, a double grouping of three notes each (6/8-time). The first beat of a rhythmic group normally receives the accent and in quadruple time the third beat gets a secondary accent. As the status of the word in a song becomes dependent on the status of the note (or notes) it is set to, it follows that words on heavy beats are more accented than words on weak beats.

It may be asked if there exists a correspondence between the choice of mood or scenery in the poem and the time and tempo of the air. Edward A. Sonnenschein in *What is Rhythm?* says that "it is a commonplace of aesthetics that each rhythm has its own particular character, which makes it appropriate for the expression of particular moods of the mind". A slow tempo, he says, tends to have a soothing and calming effect, unless the rhythm is very jerky, whereas a quick tempo is exciting.[5] Slow triple rhythm can be lulling and rocking, quick triple rhythm dancing and swinging. Similarly duple rhythm in slow tempo is different in expression from duple rhythm in quick tempo; a march ceases to be a march if we play it too fast. Deryck Cooke, who has made an interesting study of the language of music, finds that there is an intrinsic difference of expression between duple and triple time (provided tonal tensions, tempo, volume, and phrasing function do not work in the opposite way). He says that ". . . Its basic effect can be seen as the contrast between the regular, rigid, masculine rhythm of the two feet marching or running, and the looser,

[5] Edward A. Sonnenschein, *What is Rhythm?* (Oxford: Basil Blackwell, 1925), p. 4.

21

swinging or lilting, feminine rhythm of the dance . . . As a general rule we may take it that duple rhythm is more rigid and controlled, triple rhythm more relaxed and abandoned."[6] His book is concerned with art-music, but the point is general enough to be applicable to the music in the present study.

Burns was aware of such intrinsic qualities of a tune and with an unerring sensitivity he slowed down quick dance-tunes (often minor ones) to bring out new expressions (cf. Ch. 1, n. 17). Daiches says that he was thereby "able to bring out an elegiac quality that was concealed in a faster tempo",[7] but in another book he also points out that many of these fast dance-tunes had in fact originally been songs, only speeded up to be used without words as instrumental music.[8] One must be careful, however, not to separate tempo from other elements of music. Bronson points out that "we do not wring sadness out of every tune merely by slowing it down",[9] it is the interplay of mode, melodic and rhythmic structure, time and tempo that gives each tune its unique expression.

The rhythmic pattern of the tune basically coincides with the poetic metre. Here great freedom reigns, but the commonest type of folk-verse is the iambic and the dactylic. As a note can always be divided to half its note-value, additional syllables can also be packed into the two- or three-syllable foot. Words can be set to music either syllabically, that is one syllable for each note (example 3), or semi-syllabically, which is one syllable stretched over two (or more) notes. The expression of a song sometimes lies embodied in the way the words are matched to the tune. If, for example, in a lively song, the setting is syllabic, the words have to trip along with the fast tempo and be pronounced very quickly, which may then be significant for the particular effect of that song. In many cases syllabic setting is also closer to speech-rhythm.

A tune consists of equal or dotted notes, a dotted note being one which is lengthened by half its own value (indicated by a dot after the note). As long notes tend to give accentuation, a dotted note may emphasize a word or a syllable, unless the melodic contour or other aspects of the whole musical set-up should work against it. Example 1 shows that words which are stressed in the poetical and spoken rhythm ("lay", "loof", "mine", "lass") will be even more so when sung to the dotted rhythm. In undotted rhythm each word would have been equally long. There is also a difference of expression between dotted and undotted rhythms. Cooke observes that the latter has an effect "of a smooth, unimpeded flow of any particular emotion", whereas the former

---

[6] Deryck Cooke, *The Language of Music* (Oxford: OUP, 1959), p. 97.
[7] Daiches, *Robert Burns*, p. 285.
[8] David Daiches, *The Paradox of Scottish Culture: The Eighteenth-Century Experience* (London: OUP, 1964), pp. 32–33.
[9] Bronson, *The Ballad as Song*, p. 125.

allows for more tension.[10] Although the polarity between dotted and undotted rhythm is less palpable in folk-music than in art-music, it yet seems that the distinction was significant for Burns. In his musical manuscript of "Here's his health in water" (583 A) he changes undotted notes to dotted ones (see Ch. 1, n. 28), and in a letter to Thomson he complains about the tune "The Caledonian Hunt's Delight" that "to fit it with verses to suit these dotted crotchets will be a task indeed" (Letter 647).

Most ballads and folk-songs start with an anacrusis (an upbeat) and this is also true of Burns's songs; very few of them start on the beat. But Burns came to realize that there is more energy in a song which lacks the upbeat. One is immediately and emphatically launched into such a song without the kind of preparation that an upbeat provides. The impact on the ear is much more sudden and dramatic, whereas an upbeat seems to lead one into the song by the hand and give it a smoother start. Julia P. Dabney calls the style of verse that starts with anacrusis "strict verse" as opposed to "direct attack". She finds that the "use of the anacrusis imparts a certain elegance and suavity—as it were, a legato movement—to the verse". The direct attack, on the other hand, "gives a splendid momentum to the rhythmic movement, much like the first launching spring of a swimmer".[11] The effect in songs is very much the same and after some attempts Burns arrived at the same conclusion.

His first reference to the upbeat comes in April 1793. He writes to George Thomson:

That business of many of our tunes wanting at the begin^g what Fiddlers call, a starting-note, is often a rub to us poor Rhymers.—
"There's braw, braw lads in Yarrow braes,"
you may alter to
"Braw, braw lads on Yarrow braes,
"Rove among the blooming heather"—. (Letter 554)

His second version of the line is better, for it focuses the attention on the significant word "Braw" in a more direct and emphatic way. Yet, Burns's suggested change is only made as a concession to the music. He is not yet aware of the latent musical-poetical effect of a direct attack, only of the troubles it gives the "poor Rhymers". In a later letter (Sept. 1793), however, he discusses the expressive aspects of the lack of an upbeat and makes it clear that it is the "native style" of the music which must preside over the poetic:

I must premise, that the old way, & the way to give most effect, is to have no starting note, as the Fiddlers call it, but to burst at once into the pathos.—Every country girl sings—

---

[10] Cooke, p. 100.

[11] Julia P. Dabney, *The Musical Basis of Verse: A Scientific Study of the Principles of Poetic Composition* (New York: Longmans, Green and Co., 1901), p. 47.

Saw ye my *father* &c.—
I saw not &c.—

this last, to be sure hurts the poetry, "*I* saw," instead of, "I *saw*" but I am speaking of the air. (Letter 586)

This is a fine proof of Burns's sensitive ear and marvellous instinct for what is traditional and idiomatic and a fine judgement of the relative balance between the music and the poetry. In this case it is the music which has to be left intact, as so much of the expression lies there, rather than in the poetry. At a later stage, in 1794, when Burns was working with "Lassie wi' the lintwhite locks" (466) he makes his point very clear:

Leaving out the starting-note, in both tunes, has I think an effect that no regularity could counterbalance the want of.—Try

　　　{ O Roy's Wife &c.
　　　{ O Lassie wi' the lint-white locks—

and compare with

　　　{ Roy's Wife of Aldivaloch—
　　　{ Lassie wi' the lint-white locks—

does not the tameness of the prefixed syllable strike you?—In the last case, with the true furor of genius, you strike at once into the wild originality of the air; whereas in the first insipid business it is like the grating screw of the pins before the fiddle is brought in tune. (Letter 647)

A peculiar feature of Scottish airs is the so-called "Scots snap", the eccentric, jerky rhythm which is to be found especially in the strathspeys (see below) and which Collinson aptly calls "*the very life-blood of Scots musical rhythm*" (example 4).[12] It is a very energetic rhythmic figure, in which the accented beat is shorter than the unaccented. This makes one stress the first beat even more in order to make the rhythm as clear as possible. The unaccented beat is never felt as the anacrusis to the next note, which often happens in equal or dotted rhythms, and therefore this rhythmic group is very stable.[13] As the accent always falls heavy on the first beat, it also tends to affect the pronunciation of the initial consonant of the word. The quicker the air, the more energy is needed to sing the snaps and the more forceful consonants have to be spat out. Collinson finds that in a slow tempo, e.g. in Gaelic songs, which

[12] Collinson, p. 29. The conventional way of noting it is as in example 4:1, but in reality it is often much shorter, as in 4:2.
[13] Cooper and Meyer, p. 30.

also have this peculiar rhythm, the onset becomes "persuasive" rather than hard.[14] The snap is therefore a very potent element in the expression of a song in general and of words in particular.

There are three main types of tunes in Scottish music: the jig, which is of Irish origin, and has a 9/8 or 6/8 triple rhythm, the reel, in 4/4 or 2/4, which has equal notes in the notation (but not necessarily in the execution) and an even beat in a fast-tripping tempo, and the strathspey, also that in 4/4 or 2/4 but slower and with a more uneven beat and more unexpected turns in the rhythm. To the strathspey-type can also be added the Highland Gaelic tunes which, as Ernest Walker puts it, are "curiously rugged in form, wandering on in more or less vague rhythm from one phrase to the next".[15] An eighteenth-century characterization of the reels and strathspeys indicates that they were felt to express different sentiments. In 1798 Alexander Campbell writes in a "Conversation on Scotish Song": "The Athol reel is lively, and animating in a high degree. The strathspey is much slower, better accented, and more expressive in its cadence. The movements to the former are spirited, yet less graceful; while the peculiar cast of the strathspey, which generally possesses a more varied melody, besides accent, and expression, is full of sentiment and passion."[16]

iii. Melody

Scottish tunes are often described as being "wild" and "irregular", and they have a unique flavour which has caused many to wonder about their intrinsic expression. James Beattie, for instance, in 1776, found the Highland tunes full of the "wildest irregularity" and of a melancholy, which "approaches even to the terrible". The Lowland tunes, on the other hand, he found "expressive of love and tenderness, and other emotions suited to the tranquillity of pastoral life".[17] William Tytler, the author of "A Dissertation on Scottish Music", felt that the "Scots melodies contain strong expression of the passions, particularly of the melancholy kind",[18] and William Dauney, in *Ancient Scottish Melodies,* observes that

although the melodies are often equivocal in regard to key, making rapid transitions from one to another, they are, in reality, constructed upon one scale or series of

[14] Collinson, p. 65.

[15] Ernest Walker, *A History of Music in England,* 3rd rev. and enl. ed. (Oxford: Clarendon, 1952), p. 379.

[16] Alexander Campbell, *An Introduction to the History of Poetry in Scotland ... with a conversation on Scotish Song* (Edinburgh: Andrew Foulis, 1798), p. 20.

[17] Beattie, p. 483.

[18] Tytler, p. 637.

sounds; and that the reason why they have the appearance of being composed in different keys, and in different modes, and of a singular wildness and variety of their effect, is the freedom with which they wander up and down the scale, and every now and then rest upon certain parts of it, which, for the time, become principal or leading notes.[19]

In a letter Burns tells the following story:

A good many years ago a Mr Ja^s Miller, Writer in your good town, a gentleman whom, possibly, you know—was in company with our friend, Clarke; and talking of Scots music, Miller expressed an ardent ambition to be able to compose a Scots air.—Mr Clarke, partly by way of joke, told him, to keep to the black keys of the harpsichord, & preserve some kind of rhythm; & he would infallibly compose a Scots air. (Letter 646)

Wherein lies the "Scottishness" of Scots music, asks Francis Collinson, and as the first element he mentions the pentatonic, "gapped" scales.[20] These are five-tone-scales which "lack" two of the seven degrees of the heptatonic modal scales and which can be produced, just as Burns describes it, on the black keys of the piano (example 5). The "gaps" can be filled in with either major or minor degrees and each pentatonic scale is therefore potentially related to three heptatonic modes. There are seven such modes, the Ionian, Dorian, Phrygian, Lydian, Mixolydian, Aeolian, and Locrian, and each is to be recognized by the position of the semi-tones. If only one of the "missing" degrees is filled in, the scale becomes hexatonic (six tones).

Attempts were earlier made to ascribe semantic "meanings" to each of these modes, but although it is obvious that they differ widely in character and expression, statements like, the "*Aeolik* Mood is that, which, with its soft pleasing sounds, pacifyeth the Passions of the mind" and the "*Phrygian* Mood is a manly and corragious kind of Musik"[21] are now refuted. Bronson has tried to show how, in fact, each mode is easily malleable to different expressions, because it has a correspondence with other modes, and also how it is sometimes impossible to decide the mode of a tune.[22] He calls such tunes "chameleon tunes" because they "lend themselves to lively or plaintive moods with equal readiness" and he also mentions how rich Scotland is in them.[23] For that reason analyses of the specific expressions of the different modes and their relation to the lyrics will not be attempted in this study.

But what can be significant for the expression of a song is the minor or ma-

---

[19] William Dauney, *Ancient Scottish Melodies* (Edinburgh: Maitland Club, 1838), p. 175.

[20] Collinson, p. 4. Karpeles thinks that this widely-used term ("gapped" scales) should be discouraged, as it implies something incomplete and defective (Karpeles, p. 35). I have used it, however, as it makes it easier to explain the scales in a few words.

[21] Charles Butler, *The Principles of Music, in Singing and Setting: with the two-fold use thereof, ecclasiasticall and civil* (London: Iohn Haviland, 1636), p. 2.

[22] Bronson, *The Ballad as Song*, pp. 129–30.

[23] Ibid., pp. 124–25.

26

jor quality of a tune. This may be more or less pronounced as some tunes begin in the major and end in the minor, others have both minor and major notes in them. Four modes are identical, or next to identical, with the major and minor scales. These are the Ionian (major), the Mixolydian (major with a lowered seventh), the Aeolian (natural minor) and the Dorian (minor with a raised sixth). James Beattie's statement that the "*minor mode*, is found to be well adapted to a melancholy subject"[24] mirrors the common feeling that the minor mode is sad and the major happy. When connected with a lyric text the major or minor quality of the tune may be reinforced and the distinction thus have a certain bearing on the song. But it must also be remembered that rhythm and tempo are participating factors of the total expression of a song and that, to paraphrase Bronson (see above, p. 22), one does not necessarily wring sadness out of a tune merely by changing it into minor.

Another aspect of the modes which will be examined in the analyses of the songs is the difference in expression between plagal and authentic tunes. If a modal tune is cast in the authentic range, it is steadily anchored between the tonic (the first note of the scale) and its octave. In the plagal, on the other hand, the tonal centre is in the middle and the melody moves as much above as below it. It is, according to Bronson, "noticeably less secure, less firmly articulated" than the authentic, which is "more aspiring, more buoyant". He also suggests that "the Scottish fondness for the plagal range results in a greater weight or sobriety",[25] and the question may then be put if the plagal and authentic ranges have any relation to the mood or setting of the poem. When a tune lifts to the fifth of the scale in the second half, it very often turns into the plagal range if it has been authentic, or into the authentic if it has been plagal in the first. There is subsequently not only a change of register which intensifies and changes the expression of the second half of a tune, but also one of mode, for, as Bronson says, "every mode in its plagal range is identical with the authentic scale of another mode".[26]

What is also typical for the Scottish tunes is the double triad (a triad is a chord of three notes, the first, third and fifth of the scale, and it is based on the tonic). The double triad is a phrase on a major triad followed by a similar phrase on the major triad a tone lower. Another hallmark of the tunes, which may have some relation to the poem, is the "open" ending. A tune may close, not on its tonic, which is the most stable tone of the scale, but on any other note, usually the second, third, fifth, and sixth degrees. This ending is less final, and it can make a major tune take an unexpected minor twist at the end.

The shape of the melody itself, its register and its compass, its directions and

[24] Beattie, p. 450.
[25] Bronson, *The Ballad as Song*, pp. 154—55.
[26] Ibid., p. 81.

ways of moving, is fundamental to the specific expression of a song as well as to the impact of separate words. A melody may be more or less active. Some are buoyant with energy, others seem more introvert. Cooke has found that in art-music falls and rises in pitch, in major and minor, normally express respectively incoming and outgoing feelings of pleasure and pain,[27] a theory which may also be applied to the tunes of Burns's songs; an ascending melodic line, be it folk or art, is more assertive than a descending one (unless the effect of tempo and rhythm functions in the opposite way). It may then be asked what the emotive and dramatic import is of songs with tunes of decisively active or passive character, what the significance is of poetical lines lying on rising or falling melodic curves, and what the effect is of words falling on the top note of an ascending phrase. A tune may also proceed in a jerky contour with abrupt and large skips and leaps, it may have an undulating shape and move by very small intervallic steps, or it may remain more or less on the same level. Upbeats may start high or low, the former having a more energetic and emphatic expression than the latter, which gives a smoother start to the song. All these aspects, along with rhythm and form, are essential in an analysis of the songs *qua* songs, and in the following chapters the relation of Burns's lyrics and their themes to such musical aspects will be discussed.

But before proceeding to the songs a few words will be said about the nature of lyrics which are specifically written to be sung.[28] It is commonly felt that long, narrative poems or intellectual poems with abstract diction, literary devices and complex ideas are less suited to the simplicity of folk-tunes. Bruce Pattison, in *Music and Poetry of the English Renaissance* says that "... Verse for music should ... keep to broad and simple emotions. Subtlety or verbal ingenuity are almost certain to be lost on the listener: they may be introduced sparingly, but will have to be carefully placed."[29] Gavin Greig points out "that in order to give emotions as free play as possible the intellect must have little to do. Hence all literary devices that closely engage the attention should be avoided in verses intended to be sung ... Simplicity in its best and widest sense must be aimed at."[30] Both writers thus stress the emotional aspect and the need for simplicity in a song, and as we shall see the best songs of Burns are the sim-

[27] Cooke, pp. 105—06.

[28] A good account of the discussions which went on in Britain in the eighteenth century concerning the "true" union of poetry and music is found in Herbert M. Schueller, "Literature and Music as Sister Arts: An Aspect of Aesthetic Theory in Eighteenth-Century Britain", *Philological Quarterly*, 26, No. 3 (1947), 193—205; see also, as background to Burns's achievement, Kinsley, "The Music of the Heart", pp. 5—35.

[29] Bruce Pattison, *Music and Poetry of the English Renaissance* (London: Methuen, 1948), p. 142.

[30] Gavin Greig, "Song-writing", in A. Stephen Wilson, *Words Wooing Music* (Aberdeen: John Rae Smith, 1890), p. xxxviii.

ple ones in which emotions are expressed. Similarly the tune chosen for lyric setting requires simplicity; length and complexity muddle directness and clarity of text, and a long, elaborate tune is less flexible to changing sentiments within a lyric and tends to overpower it.

Certainly Burns would have agreed with the ideas put forth by John Aikin in *Essay on Song-Writing* (cf. above, p. 13). Aikin finds that "emotions of tenderness and gaiety are peculiarly adapted to song-writing"[31] and he stresses the importance of simplicity in a song: "A succession of new ideas started in every line, just touched upon, and immediately lost, distracts the attention, and enfeebles the effect of the whole; and amidst the profusion of ornament, real elegance and beauty is overwhelmed."[32] A passage from a letter to George Thomson shows that Burns was well aware of the need for simplicity in a song (although not always in practice). He says that "of pathos, Sentiment, & Point, you are a compleat judge; but there is a quality more necessary than either, in a Song, & which is the very essence of a Ballad, I mean Simplicity—now, if I mistake not, this last feature you are a little apt to sacrifice to the foregoing" (Letter 554).

Julia P. Dabney holds that poetry of itself is a species of music. She finds that the "merit of true poetry lies largely in its suggestiveness, a suggestiveness only to be fully brought home by oral interpretation",[33] or, it might be added, by musical interpretation. But there is also a suggestiveness in music, and it is here that the two elements meet. When Burns first heard a tune he tried to capture its dominant sentiment and for that "suggested" sentiment write a lyric which was in unison with it. Greig believes that an alliance between text and tune "involves a compromise, a limitation of function and aim on both sides. Absolute music must be purely instrumental; and the highest forms of poetry refuse to be sung".[34] But such an alliance also has another important function: music and words may complement each other so that the whole becomes greater than the sum of its two parts.

Bronson has shown that there are certain restrictions in the setting of words to music. As a folk-tune is short and repeats itself over and over again, "at the same emotional pitch, in unvarying statement" it follows that it responds easily to a "series of parallel expressions of an emotion—a single emotion, whether joy or sadness, love or grief—where the element of story is withheld".[35] From this statement the conclusion should not be drawn, however, that no emotional change can take place in the lyric without requiring a change in the music as

[31] Aikin, p. 12.

[32] Ibid., p. 201.

[33] Dabney, p. 17.

[34] Gavin Greig, *Folk-song in Buchan and Folk-song of the North-east* (Hatboro, Pa.: Folklore Associates, 1963), p. 19.

[35] Bronson, "Some Aspects of Music and Literature", pp. 52—53.

well. The range of emotions can in fact be very wide, and yet not inimical to the nature of folk-tunes. The "chameleon quality" of Scottish folk-tunes has already been discussed in this chapter (see above, "Melody") and it is just that quality which allows the same air to be sad or gay or spirited depending on its speed and on what words are set to it. Bronson mentions the tune "Hey tutti taiti" as a good example of this. This tune was originally connected with a cheerful drinking-song ("Landlady count the lawin", 206), but to which Burns later set his patriotic and powerful "Robert Bruce's March to Bannockburn" (425) and Lady Nairne her tender "Land of the Leal".[36] It is also this aspect of the Scottish tunes which allows for changes of the emotional register within the same song, depending on how the words and what words are joined to them. As a contemporary view on the flexibility of a tune I quote James Beattie, as Burns had read his essay *On Poetry & Music*:

The change of the poet's ideas, provided the subject continue nearly the same, does not always require a change of the music: and if critics have ever determined otherwise, they were led into the mistake, by supposing, what every musician knows to be absurd, that, in fitting verses to a tune, or a tune to verses, it is more necessary, that *particular words* should have *particular notes* adapted to them, than that the *general tenor* of the music should accord with the *general nature* of the sentiments.[37]

---

[36] Bronson, "Some Aspects of Music and Literature", p. 54.
[37] Beattie, p. 463.

30

Chapter 3

Love and the Lassies

The majority of Burns's songs deal with love, love seen from the poet's point of view or love seen through the eyes of one of the lovers. There are conventional pieces, droll and humorous scenes, young love, mature love, and erotic love. There are love-songs where the emphasis lies on sentiment, others where it lies on character or on action. Among all these songs we find Burns's most interesting and exciting characters. These are his young girls in love and particularly those who speak for themselves in the songs. Here Burns shows an extraordinary psychological insight into the feminine mind and as Christina Keith points out, at the time he wrote them he had "had great experience of girls, at any rate of the particular girl he had chosen as his type".[1] These girls display a considerable amount of independence, of self-confidence, of self-knowledge, and of knowledge of the world. Their world is love, and love exclusively, but into this world they grow and through love they grow, from the first stage of girlhood and innocence into womanhood and experience. They come into conflict with convention and the code of female behaviour and with their parents' opinions, but in all situations they show strength of mind and individuality. A passive woman who lets herself be subdued cannot be found among these young women. Furthermore, as Christina Keith has shown,[2] Burns carried on the tradition of the Scottish folk-songs and ballads in which free love had managed to survive in spite of the Reformation and John Knox's attack on women. The Kirk had an iron grip on the people and on women, who had a very low status. Love flourished, however, where the Kirk could not reach it, in the Borders and in the Highlands, and with it the free and independent woman. In these songs we find the women of the old Scotland, women who "were captivating, free and elegant, without the remotest shadow of subjection".[3]

The youngest and most innocent of these girls is to be found in "Tam Glen" (236), a song which gives a portrait of a highly infatuated girl who is totally engrossed in the thoughts of her lover. Excitedly, she chatters away without stop about her dear Tam Glen, naively she believes in superstitious omens, and

[1] Keith, *The Russet Coat*, p. 147.
[2] Ibid., pp. 205—06.
[3] Ibid., pp. 198—99.

with growing self-confidence she reacts against her parents' opinions. The situation is common enough: the mother warns her against flattering men and the father wants her to marry for money. She listens to neither for the only advice she wants to hear is to marry Tam Glen. With the impatience of a very young girl in love, she begs and bribes her sister:

> Come counsel, dear Tittie, don't tarry;
> I'll gie you my bonie black hen,
> Gif ye will advise me to Marry
> The lad I lo'e dearly, Tam Glen.—

Her character, her girlishness and her state of mind with its agitation and restlessness is conveyed through words and music. The quick flight of her thoughts and the intensity of her chatter lie embodied in the quick tempo of the tune (the 9/8-time is suggestive of this) and in the syllabic setting for the undotted notes, which makes one pronounce each word quickly and vigorously and with equal force. Kinsley notes the preoccupation with the name and also how the "girl's persistent chatter" is sustained by the melody. She speaks uninterruptedly, her heart seems to beat quickly, and she has hardly time to take a breath before she starts talking again. The shortness of the tune (it is only four bars long), the monotonous melody and the even rhythm captures this very well. Only at the end of the second and fourth bars does the tune come to a rest on a crotchet and on these cadences the repeated name of Tam Glen and its rhymes fall.

At one point in each stanza there is an intensification of the girl's emotions. This happens in the last bar, where the melody emphatically rises. There is a large and unexpected upward skip to the highest note of the tune followed by a gradual descent to the tonic (example 6). This feature of the tune reinforces the climax of the fourth lines of each stanza and, as the mode is minor, it lends them a sense of despair and exasperation. But there is also irritation and impatience in the expression and the high note brings out the important question words "what", "when" and "wha". These lines are also the keys to the girl's state of mind. Young as she seems and new as the sensation is to her, she is full of wonder, questions and impatience: *"what* will I do", *"wha* can think sae" and *"wha* will I get".

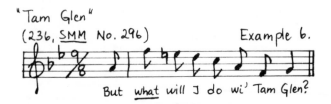

"Tam Glen"
(236, SMM No. 296)   Example 6.

But what will I do wi' Tam Glen?

Another young, inexperienced but less impatient girl appears in "I'm o'er young to Marry Yet" (195), a more uncomplicated song with humorous implications. This girl is being courted by a man somewhat older than herself, but she rejects him, claiming that she is too young to marry. Yet she is intelligent—and witty—enough to see that it will not be long before she is ready to say yes. She measures time by the seasons, and half a year, from winter to summer, is what she believes she needs to be old enough to marry. The song is spun around the contrasts between winter and summer, young and old, mother's child and man's woman, innocence and experience, the present and the future. The girl is now her mother's "ae bairn" (*only child*), she is "o'er young", and "o'er young" is repeated four times in the chorus, it is "winter" and "frosty" and both words are emphasized through the rise in the melody. But what will come is implied strongly enough in the last stanza of the song:

> Fu' loud and shill the frosty wind
>   Blaws thro' the leafless timmer, Sir;   *trees*
> But if ye come this gate again,
>   I'll aulder be gin simmer, Sir.   *towards*

The light note of the song is struck already in the old chorus from which Burns took his start (*Notes,* p. 25), and the skittish, cheerful and innocent character of the young girl is suggested in the light-tripping reel-tune, the even rhythm, the quick tempo, the high register, the rising phrases, and the major mode. Crawford acknowledges the importance of the tune and says that "the words and music combine to give us a girl's mood shortly after puberty—shy, blushing, yet full of the knowledge of what she is and what she must become".[4]

In the first line of the song ("I am my mammy's ae bairn") the significance and implications of the word "ae" are emphasized in the musical context. It emphatically falls on a rising melodic line as well as on two notes in the otherwise syllabic setting of the song. The fact that the girl is her mother's only child is one of the reasons she gives to the man for not marrying him, and therefore " 'twad be a sin / To tak me frae my mammy yet". The other reason for her denial of the man is that she shudders at the thought of creeping into bed with him: "And lying in a *man's* bed, / I'm fley'd it make me irie, Sir" (*afraid; frightened*). In this example (from stanza 1) "man's" falls on two notes, emphasizing an implied antithesis—to lie in a man's bed and not in one's own—and in stanza 2 ("And you an' I in ae bed, / In trowth, I dare na venture, Sir") the word "ae" is accented. A man and one bed, that is a collocation which is quite beyond her field of experience.

The "Sir" at the end of every second line has several functions. It makes the song more personal (the girl addresses one particular man) at the same time as

---

[4] Crawford, p. 304.

it shows the girl's respect for the older man, but the word is also needed for technical reasons. Without it the cadence would end rather heavily on "wiinter", 'ti-immer" etc. Daiches notes this and says that "the diction flows with a happy directness and a fine dramatic feeling, while the monosyllable 'Sir' provides just what the poem needs to bring the rhythms of the reel into the diction and fit the piece perfectly to its tune".[5]

A girl who ventures into bed with a man with less hesitation is "the sleepy bit lassie" in "The Taylor fell thro' the bed, &c." (286). "She thought that a Taylor could do her nae ill" and once she has been initiated she joyfully sings out her longing and her passion. The song has a wide register and, as Kinsley points out, it moves "from comedy through passion to longing, and a last touch of comedy". Only the second and fourth stanzas are Burns's own (*Notes*, p. 43), but, as Kinsley notes, these, and the change in the third stanza from the traditional "The night it is short and the day it is lang, / It's a dear-won tipence to lie wi' a man" to "The day it is short and the night it is lang, / The dearest siller that ever I wan" completely change the character of the song and the girl. Her frank and spontaneous passion now successfully corresponds to the free swing of the tune. It is major and has a dotted 6/8 rhythm which, along with the upward leap of an octave in the first and third bars, both enlivens the comical note in the song and expresses the girl's uninhibited joy in love-making.

Very free and independent for her eighteen years, mature and full of opposition against her parents is the girl of "O, for ane and twenty Tam" (363). She will not be oppressed by them any longer, nor will she marry a fool for his money. She knows her worth and as soon as she comes of age ("ane and twenty") she will marry the boy she loves. Her maturity and strength is expressed through both text and tune. The melancholy high part with its stronger minor quality, its small intervals and intensifying upward direction enhances the girl's bitter feelings against her parents, expressed in the first stanza: "They snool me sair, and haud me down, / And gar me look like bluntie, Tam" (snool *snub*; sair *sore*; haud *hold*; gar *make*; bluntie *fool*). It also makes her opposition, expressed in the more relaxed chorus, psychologically logical. This girl has none of the worries of the girl in "Tam Glen", she is not dependent on anybody, and in the last stanza she gives her hand in pledge to the boy: "But hearst thou, laddie, there's my loof, / I'm thine at ane and twenty, Tam!" (*hand given in pledge*). The girl in "Tam Glen" is on her way to self-confidence and independence, but she still feels that "to anger them a' is a pity" (meaning her parents) and she needs her sister's support. The tune of "O for ane" is slow (see below) and much less excited than that of "Tam Glen". The emphatic high starts of the upbeats in the chorus ("*An* O", "*An* hey") give the girl's words a

---

[5] Daiches, *Robert Burns,* p. 296.

sense of conviction. She takes her time and rests on the cadences with the repeated "twenty Tam", and there is also a refrain-line in each stanza and a chorus to give the song a more balanced expression. Burns conceived of this song as fairly slow and he was not pleased with the setting in *SMM* (where it is marked as "canty" *lively*). In a letter to Thomson he writes: "but if you will get any of our ancienter Scots Fiddler to play you, *in Strathspey time* (my italics), 'The Moudiewort,' (that is the name of the air) I think it will delight you" (Letter 644). The younger girl in "Tam Glen" is restlessly babbling on with no sense of pause anywhere: "She keeps on at it too—as they do—dinning the name at you in verse after verse", as Christina Keith puts it.[6] Her conversation with her sister is intimate, worried, secret and whispering, whereas the girl in "O for ane" is critical, extrovert, straightforward and free.

She shares her strength of character with the girl in "Country Lassie" (369). Just like her this girl is not prepared to listen to the materialistic and moral advice of her elders or let them decide for her, and she knows that "the tender heart o' leesome loove, / The gowd and siller canna buy" (*dear love*). The poem is set to a beautiful, slightly melancholy tune, but the length and complexity of the poem, along with its dialogue form, make the ties between text and tune seem weaker in this song and allow less insight into character.

"The gallant Weaver" (380) also has the theme of the conflict between love and money but is less dramatic than the songs discussed above. Its major tune is gently undulating, its tempo is slow, and the rhythm alternates smoothly between crotchets and quavers. The opening scene is all pleasantness, the "Cart rins rowin to the sea, / By mony a flower and spreading tree" (*rolling*), and with conviction and confidence the girl calmly sings:

> My daddie sign'd my tocher-band   *marriage-settlement*
> To gie the lad that has the land,
> But to my heart I'll add my hand
> And give it to the Weaver.—

Because of the musical pattern there is no sense of opposition or excitement in the third line of the quoted stanza. The air flows on at the same unvaried pace, having almost the same melodic curve here as for the first line. Emotional peaks are levelled out, and the impression is conveyed that this girl knows what she wants and that a parental decision cannot upset her or make her change her mind. This optimism is reinforced by the last stanza which lies on the high part of the tune, has a repetitional pattern and positive words like "rejoice" and "delight".

Another girl who is confronted with a materialistic love is the girl in "My Tochers the Jewel" (345). The conflict in this song does not lie between the girl

---

[6] Keith, *The Russet Coat,* p. 147.

and her parents, but within the girl herself, for she has seen through her lover: "My laddie's sae meikle in love wi' the siller, / He canna hae luve to spare for me" (*much*). She presents this situation in the first half-stanza with a striking antithesis between "O meikle thinks my Luve o' my beauty" and the bitter truth of "But little thinks my Luve, I ken brawlie, / My tocher's the jewel has charms for him" (*know well; dowry*). This last line is intensified through the lift in the tune followed by a descent. There is melancholy and sadness in the girl's voice, an expression which is conveyed entirely by the slow, minor tune. In the second stanza she shows that she has insight and strength, and she despises the money-seeking lover: "But an ye be crafty, I am cunnin, / Sae ye wi' anither your fortune maun try" (an *if*; maun *must*). As Kinsley points out the song is not quite homogeneous as the last half stanza is old and not made an organic part of the song.

"When she can ben she bobbed" (362) is not a song about or by a lassie as much as to a lassie. The singer (probably a man) wants to implant in the girl's mind just those values which we have seen are held high by the young girls in the other songs:

> O never look down, my lassie at a',
> O never look down, my lassie at a';
> Thy lips are as sweet and thy figure compleat,
> As the finest dame in castle or ha'.—

As noted by Kinsley, Burns took his start (lines 1—6) from a traditional song which presents a flirtatious laird who spites his wife for the collier lassie and "the lass in the stable". Burns changes the character of this man and makes him the true lover who chooses the collier lassie for love, instead of the wealthy "dochter of a lord" for her money. The girl, who is presented as shy and submissive in the first, traditional stanza ("O when she cam ben she bobbed fu' law" *indoors*; *curtseyed very low*), is then told to keep her head high and be proud, for her worth lies not in her economic status. The tune is light and lilting (6/8-time and major) but also emphatic with its snaps and upward skips and runs. This gives weight to the man's words, yet keeps the song at a light-hearted level. The lift of an octave in the second two-bar phrase should be noticed, for it gives a new intensification to the repetition in the second line of each stanza which passes unnoticed if the song is read.

A young girl's wishes might not only conflict with the expectations of the parents, as in many of the songs above, but also with society's claims for virtue, innocence and honour. In "Wha is that at my bower door?" (356) the girl makes strong attempts to resist the man, as it is expected of her, but the song shows her slowly yielding to him, only a little anxious that anybody will know. The idea of the dialogue-form of the song is very old and Burns had an immediate model in a broadside. As pointed out by Kinsley, this has the same structure, with questions and answers, as Burns's own song, but lacks the humour and insight into character:

> Who's that at my chamber door?
> And who but I? quoth Finlay.
> Lown carle, come no further.   *rascal fellow*
> Indeed not I, quoth Finlay.

(Quoted by Kinsley)

From this old broadside stanza and in the tradition of the night-visiting songs Burns develops the theme in his own way, creating, with a strong sense of humour, a "carle" who is self-assured, masculine and straightforward in his attempts to be let in by the girl:

> Wha is that at my bower-door?
> O wha is it but Findlay;
> Then gae your gate, ye'se nae be here!   *go your way*
> Indeed maun I, quo' Findlay.—   *must; said*

Findlay's character remains constant throughout the song. His lines are only slightly varied with a touch of humour, as he teasingly takes up the preceding words of the girl: "In my bower *if ye should stay, / Let me stay,* quo' Findlay" or "Here this night *if ye remain, / I'll remain,* quo' Findlay". He sets out with one intention—to make the girl let him in—and he makes no attempts to conceal this. He is certain that her hesitation is only a conventional attitude and that his honest, but slightly provoking manner will force her into a quicker decision. She, in turn, shows that she knows perfectly well what it is all about. She is on her guard and puts Findlay on trial by being seemingly resistant. "Before the morn ye'll work mischief", she says and goes on:

> Gif I rise and let you in,
> Let me in, quo' Findlay;
> Ye'll keep me waukin wi' your din;
> Indeed will I, quo' Findlay.—

Crawford describes the situation this way: "From the very start, despite all appearances to the contrary, she has wanted to let Findlay into the bower, and she ends as absolute mistress of the situation. Findlay has made a binding promise to her (to be secret)—that is, he has yielded to her femininity; and the joke is that he thinks that *he* has conquered her!"[7]

The tune suits the poem perfectly. It has a simplicity which allows the oppositions to be exposed, the oppositions between the questions and answers, between the apparent change in the girl's attitude and the constancy in Findlay's, and between her worries and his self-confidence. It is short, consisting of only eight bars, where one bar in the music corresponds to one line in

---

[7] Crawford, p. 295.

the lyric. Significantly the girl's words are sung to arched or descending phrases, whereas Findlay's lie on the arched or more aggressive ascending ones (example 7). Especially the second and sixth bars (corresponding to the second line of each stanza) are very emphatic in their assertive upward direction. This becomes the climax of each stanza and helps to express the joy Findlay takes in challenging the girl's female code of coyness. It is also the point where he teases her by repeating her words (see above). A sense of strength and assurance is also embodied in the dotted four-beat rhythm of the tune and in the lack of an upbeat (example 7). The potency of the "direct attack" on "*Wha* is that", "*What* mak ye", "*Gif* I rise" brings out a tone of irritation in the attitude of the girl. This points to a strong attempt to cover up the desire to let him in, but it is also a sign of her independence. The girl is, as has been pointed out, not completely in Findlay's power.

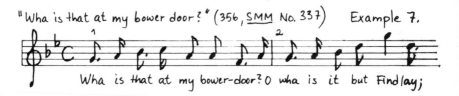

"Wha is that at my bower door?" (356, SMM No. 337)   Example 7.

Wha is that at my bower-door? O wha is it but Findlay;

Even more illustrative of this double-standard of morality is the "Scotish Ballad" (503). In this song it is very obvious how the girl tries to cover up her real feelings by keeping up a pretence of irritation and haughtiness. Yet she knows her feminine influence and when she risks the loss of her lover she is quick to act. Passivity is not a feature of Burns's heroines. Thornton asserts that "never was there a girl more confident of her charm or more able to turn her lover inside out by teasing".[8] The song has a very human humour and touch of subtle irony, and it is set to a tune of splendid momentum and liveliness. With gentleness Burns takes the ardent lover and the proud girl through a development where, as Kinsley puts it, "she begins in the pretences of the conventionally indifferent mistress, and ends by accepting her suitor—though with the humorous understatement characteristic of the Scots", and where "he begins with the traditional protestations of the sophisticated lover, falls back on appeals to greed and ambition, and in the end betrays a natural, comically desperate passion".

The irony in the handling of the characters and the pathetic overstatement in the love-effusions of the boy is to a great extent embodied in the way the words are set to the music. The middle-cadence in the second two-bar phrase (b) is an ascending line ending on a long dotted crotchet. The words falling on this note

[8] Thornton, *The Tuneful Flame,* p. 10.

are subsequently prolonged, and dimensions and implications are brought out which cannot be heard in a read version (example 8). There is irritation in the girl's first lines: "Last May a braw wooer cam down the lang glen, / And sair wi' his love he did *deave me*" (*handsome; deafen*), and mocking despise in her rendering of the boy's pathetic words: "He spak o' the darts in my bonie black een, / And vow'd for my love he was *dying*". Her incisive answers to the boy fall on the emphatic rise in the third two-bar phrase (c), and the rise-fall followed by a dotted upward leap from the fifth to the tonic expresses the energy which the girl needs to convince herself and him of her indifference (example 8). She protests, "I said, there was *naething* I hated like men", and her "naething" is saucily spat out on this upward leap. However, already in the second stanza it is clear that she is desperately trying to keep up pretences ("I said, he might die when he liked for JEAN— / The Lord forgie me for lying, for lying") and in the third stanza she reveals that she has some feelings for the boy ("I never loot on that I kend it, or car'd" *showed; was aware of*).

"Scotish Ballad" (503, <u>SMM</u> No. 522) Example 8.

And sair wi' his love he did <u>deave</u> me; I <u>said</u>, there was naething
... My wooer he <u>caper'd</u>

In these three opening stanzas the first two phrases (a + b) of the tune are devoted to the boy and the last three (c + d + e) to the girl. The contrast between the two, thus reinforced by the music, is also emphasized by her resolute "I *said*" and "I *never*", falling on the rise up to the dotted tonic, which prolongs and accents the verbs (example 8). The irony lies in the opposition between what she says and what she actually feels, and the implications are obvious: she says one thing, but means and feels another. As the story proceeds it is the lover's turn to pretend, and being close (as she believes) to losing him, the girl has to act. She gives him a wink and "My wooer he caper'd as he'd been in drink, / And vow'd I was his dear lassie, dear lassie". Here the leap in the first bar of c makes the verb "caper'd" illustrative of the physical demonstration of the lover's joy. Crawford speaks in terms of "character, motive and mask" about this song,[9] and if the mask was indifference with the girl at the beginning, it has now developed into irony and humour. In the last stanza the boy is back

[9] Crawford, p. 300.

to the passion of the first part of the song, but the girl's answer this time expresses compassionate understatement:

> He begged, for Gudesake! I wad be his wife,
> Or else I wad kill him wi' sorrow:
> So e'en to preserve the poor body in life,   *simply*
> I think I maun wed him tomorrow, tomorrow,   *must*
> I think I maun wed him tomorrow.—

The songs discussed so far have been songs of courtship. They have caught the young girls in the act of choosing (or refusing) a lover or a husband, and they have thrown light on the conflicts which might then arise. There has been a stress on personal strength, self-confidence and independence more than on the actual feelings of love. Some of the songs have been light-hearted, suggesting young girls, others have been humorous and most of them have been set to brisk, extrovert tunes. In another group of songs the themes are spun around longing and affectionate love, the relationships are more definitely established and the tunes are of a reflective character. In his essay on different types of folk-songs Gavin Greig makes a distinction between "apostrophic", introspective love-songs, and biographic, narrative ones,[10] a distinction which applies very well to the songs in the following. To the latter group belong "My Harry was a Gallant gay" (164) and "Wae is my heart" (582) in which the girls speak about their love and their longing rather than addressing themselves straight to the beloved. The apostrophic songs, on the other hand, represent "the higher kind of lyric where the lover utters his own feelings in direct appeal to the object of his adoration". Songs of this type are the musical and lyrical translation of a central feeling and as Greig puts it, they give "unlimited scope for intensity of feeling and expression".[11]

Such a song is "For the sake o' Somebody" (566) in which a most generous and tender love is expressed, a love which is not seeking its own ends but is directed to the beloved person. There is a continuous return to the word "somebody" and a preoccupation of thought around this person. The lyric is beautifully suited to the structure, rhythm and melody of the tune, and the emotional dimensions of the song cannot be understood if text and tune are not considered together as one unity.

The tune consists of two almost identical sections, ab + a^{1}b, where a^1 lacks the upbeats and also has a heavier rhythm with longer first and third beats. In a and a^1 the phrases have an upward direction and the same melody is repeated twice, but the second time one fifth higher (example 9). This lift is strongly intensifying, and with his instinctive perception of the inherent expression of the tune Burns makes the lyrical meaning in both stanzas correspond to it:

[10] Greig, *Folk-song in Buchan and Folk-song of the North-east*, p. 34.
[11] Ibid.

> My heart is sair, I dare na tell,   *sad*
> My heart is sair for Somebody;
>
> . . . .
>
> Ye Powers that smile on virtuous love,
> O, sweetly smile on Somebody!
>
> . . . .

Whereas the first line is tentative, the second is more definite and more passionate: "My heart is sair" not for anybody, but for "Somebody", and "Ye Powers that smile" on all lovers, smile especially on "Somebody". In both stanzas one word is repeated in both lines to hold them more firmly together ("sair" and "smile"). On the descent in b the girl gives proof of her love: she could "wake a winter-night" for her lover (stanza 1) and she bids the heavenly powers to keep him from danger (stanza 2).

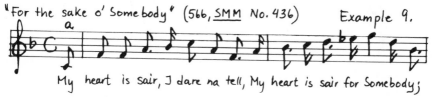

"For the sake o' Somebody" (566, SMM No. 436)   Example 9.

My heart is sair, J dare na tell, My heart is sair for Somebody;

For the second half of the tune there is a refrain with the change of the rhythm in a^1. As the rhythmical swing in the music is stronger here, the first and third beats being heavier, these lines seem more extrovert, and more overflowing with the joy of love. But the four-beat lilt and the arched melodic contour is also very expressive of sighing and yearning, and the intensity of the long close *o* of "*Ohon*" (often an expression of lament) and "*Ohey*" gives added emphasis to these feelings. The refrain-lines lead up to the protestation in the last couplet of each stanza, "I could range the warld round" and "I wad do—what wad I not", and this "For the sake o' Somebody". The fusion of the two arts, poetry and music, is most perfect in this song. The generous love and the passionate longing is embodied in both text and tune, and the simplicity and sensitivity with which the one is coupled to the other makes the song an organic whole, where each part is dependent on and enhanced by the other.

Another apostrophic song is "Ay waukin O" (287),[12] the lyrical and musical

---

[12] The original of this song was probably the following fragment collected by Herd and quoted by Kinsley:

> O wat, wat—O wat and weary!
> Sleep I can get nane
> For thinking on my deary.
> A' the night I wak,
> A' the day I weary,
> Sleep I can get nane
> For thinking on my dearie.

expression of a young girl lying awake at night, unable to sleep for thoughts of her dearie. Her longing, her unrest, her infatuation, her sadness, and her weariness, all this lies embodied in the short lyric and in its tune. The structure, the diction and the tonal language are extremely simple and nothing seems superfluous in this song. Through very small means it captures the desolate situation like a Japanese lyric, and the song itself is like a weary sigh.

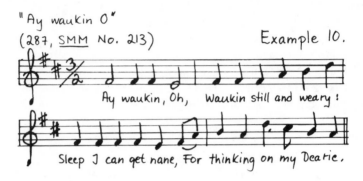

"Ay waukin O"
(287, SMM No. 213) Example 10.

Ay waukin, Oh, Waukin still and weary!

Sleep I can get nane, For thinking on my Dearie.

The chorus expresses the girl's longing, her melancholy and her sighing. On two long notes (minims) the "Ay" and the "Oh" fall, being the utterance of her love-sick heart. The minor melody drops here, enhancing that sadness, but it rises in the second bar (taking line 2) as if to express her impatience and her unrest. In the third bar it monotonously repeats the same note four times before it falls again (line 3). It finally reaches its peak in the rise of the last bar, reinforcing the intensity of the girl's feelings (example 10). The stanzas contain the thoughts occupying the girl's mind and keeping her awake. The second (see below) is only a variation of the chorus and the other two are impressionistic lines, capturing the tired thoughts passing through her mind:

> When I sleep I dream,
>> When I wauk I'm irie;   *melancholy*
> Sleep I can get nane,
>> For thinking on my Dearie.—

The music lies higher here, it has more dotted notes and seems to embody her unrest and excitement. But each poetical line is sung to a falling melodic phrase, each one starting anew as if it is an effort for the girl to express her thoughts, tired and sad as she is.

A narrative variant of the same theme is "How lang and dreary is the night" (459) of which the first version (without the chorus) appeared in *SMM*. The second version, with a chorus and set to another tune, was sent to Thomson. This song, however, lacks the simplicity and concentrated emotional impact of "Ay waukin O". Its tune is more active with melodic rises, a large upward skip in the first bar and a dotted rhythm. As it is decidedly major it also fails to convey the sadness expressed in the lyric. The song is not a naked direct expression of a longing heart as "Ay waukin O" is, but the lyrical expansion about this feeling.

In the narrative "My Harry was a Gallant gay" (164) [13] the theme of longing and sadness is opposed to that of strength and vengeance. There are tensions within the girl of her tender feelings towards Highland Harry and of her bitter feelings toward those who saw to his banishment, and these tensions are embodied both in the tune and in the poetical interpretation of the tune. The predominant thought in the girl's mind is that of Highland Harry's return home, and in the refrain it is kept alive throughout the whole song. The form of the tune is abcb[1], where ab takes the stanzas and cb[1] the chorus. Burns has followed the musical structure with the repeated b-phrase and connected his own stanzas with the theme of the old chorus (*Notes*, p. 42) by letting each last line take up the refrain of the latter:

a	My Harry was a gallant gay, Fu' stately strade he on the plain;
b	But now he's banish'd far awa, I'll never see him *back again*.
c	O for him back again, O for him back again,
b[1]	I wad gie a' Knockhaspie's land For Highland Harry *back again*.

In the chorus the girl's emotions intensify and get unbounded sway. At this point the tune changes register (it lifts by an octave) and the long first beat for "O" (n.b. the expressive lack of the upbeat) embodies all her unfulfilled longing.

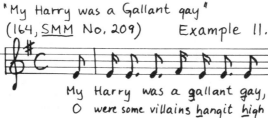

"My Harry was a Gallant gay"
(164, SMM No. 209)   Example 11.

My Harry was a gallant gay,
O were some villains hangit high

With its interplay of dotted notes and snaps, its limited tonal material (the scale is pentatonic and bars 1 and 5 are built up on the tonic) and its assertive

---

[13] This song could also be classified as a political song. Daiches points out that "almost any song in which a woman laments her dead or departed Highland lover can be said to have Jacobite overtones". David Daiches, "Robert Burns and Jacobite Song", *Critical Essays on Robert Burns*, ed. Donald A. Low (London: Routledge, 1975), p. 145.

authentic range the tune is very powerful. All this is particularly effective in the first lines of the first and last stanzas, where the snaps accent the alliterations and make the words sound forceful and fierce (example 11). There is pride in the girl's voice when she sings, "My Harry was a gallant gay, / Fu' stately strade he on the plain", and for "stately" the tune makes a large upward leap, emphasizing that word. The alliteration in "*stately strade*" also adds to the sense of power as it helps to accent the beat. But the girl's happy reverie comes to a sudden end in line 3, where she bursts out, "*But now* he's banish'd far awa". Dramatically the tune now lifts and rises to the top note, before it descends into the refrain.

In the second stanza the girl's sadness is expressed. The descent of the tune in bar 2 here becomes finely expressive of the despondency in "I wander dowie up the glen" (*sad*), as if she slowly drops her head. The stanza is a good example of the expressive flexibility of a tune. From having been powerful in the first stanza it now responds to the more lyrical expression of the words. In the last stanza the girl gathers up strength and its first half expresses suppressed anger and threat. On the melodic ascent in b, however, she cheers up at the thought of seeing her lover again: "Then I might see the joyfu' sight, / My Highlan Harry back again".

"Jamie come try me" (295)[14] also expresses the longing of a girl, but is more purely a song of the senses and a song of the passions. It is an interpretation of emotions only and says nothing about the circumstances around these emotions. It "calls up a picture of someone 'just waiting to be asked'—breathless with desire, and almost beseeching Jamie to take the first step", as Crawford puts it.[15] The contents, language and structure of the lyric in combination with the character of the tune also suggest a slightly older girl than the ones in the songs discussed above.

The impact of the song is largely dependent on the tune, and the emotional connotations of the words can only be fully understood if the song is sung. The lyric has a very tightly knit structure which is moulded on that of the tune. At five places the two-bar phrases end on a minim and a crotchet, an ending which carries the repeated "try me" and its rhymes. The three remaining phrases have, melodically and rhythmically, a less final character. They take the repeated "love", and as these musical phrases more definitely lead on to the next, the poetical lines are correspondingly subordinate clauses leading onto the following main clause. The chorus introduces the theme round which the two stanzas are spun:

[14] "This air is Oswald's; the song is mine" (*Notes,* p. 45), an unambiguous evidence of Burns's authorship, which Kinsley has completely missed out when he argues that the song is by Burns on the basis of its "finished simplicity".

[15] Crawford, p. 305.

Jamie come try me,	a
Jamie come try me,	a
If thou would win my love	b
Jamie come try me.	a
If thou should ask my love,	b
Could I deny thee?	a
If thou would win my love,	b
Jamie come try me.	a

The first "Jamie come try me" is sung on an assertively ascending melodic line going from the tonic to its octave. It lacks the upbeat which makes the invitation more direct and straightforward. After this first attempt the girl becomes sensuous and alluring and her words are sung in a low register and with less directness (the melodic curve is now arched). Then there is a sudden tone of despair in her tune. It leaps up one octave and on this high note the word "if" falls. It jumps down again, but ascends from there and comes back to the last "Jamie come try me". This time it lies very high and therefore has a stronger intensity (example 12).

"Jamie come try me" (295, SMM No. 229)   Example 12.

The stanzas, set to the second half of the tune, are spun round the if-questions and the tune in this section remains in the high register, giving more emphasis to these questions. For "Could I deny thee?" and "Wha could espy thee?" the melody rises, after which there is a return to the refrain of the song which is now sung to a passively descending melodic line: it is the last appeal, it is the least forceful, yet the snaps give it a certain urgency.

On the printed page this simple poem reveals very little of its emotional overtones. The sensuality, the urgent and alluring appeal, the intensity of the questions, the underlying despair, the wide emotional range of the song; all this lies embodied in the tune with its slow tempo, its great range, its melodic contour and the gentle lilt of the triple rhythm. One would never read the song as slowly as one can sing it, and one would not rest so pleadingly on "try",

45

"deny" and "espy". A reading of the lyric becomes tediously regular, particularly because of the repetitions.

Another song which is even more lifeless and stereotype in print is "Stay, my Charmer, can you leave me?" (197). Sung to its tune, however, it has an emotional dimension which the words alone are not capable of conveying. The song is about the cruelty of love:

> Stay, my Charmer, can you leave me;
> Cruel, cruel to deceive me!
> Well you know how much you grieve me:
>   Cruel Charmer, can you go!
>   Cruel Charmer, can you go!

The first two lines sound trite and conventional without their beautiful melodic lines, but when delivered in music they display the conflicting emotions within the woman. The melodic contour is for the first line passively descending and the plea to stay is filled with a feeling of resignation and hopelessness. But in the second line the despised woman gets excited at the thought of the deceiver: the melody changes direction and now emphatically rises. It is the cruelty of the committed "crime" which is the overwhelming feeling and the word "cruel" is repeated twice, the second time more incisively on the top note of the rising line. The word comes back, in lines 4 and 5, but are then connected with "Charmer". Line 4 is set to a descending phrase, it is passive, accepting facts, whereas line 5 is a sudden outburst of pain making the end of the song highly dramatic. There is an abrupt change of register of an octave and a fourth and a rise at the end of the phrase which changes the mechanical repetition of "Cruel Charmer, can you go!" into a kind of haunting thought in the lover's mind. The impact of the second stanza is weaker because of its stilted language and repeated "by". But the music levels out the grossest effects of this and lends different colours to each line. What was said about the repeated "cruel" in lines 4 and 5 applies equally to "do not" in lines 9 and 10.

"Wae is my heart" (582) is also a song about the pains of love, although presented with more pretentiousness than the songs above. The grief felt by the girl is heightened by the slow tune with its falling contour and dramatic upward leap in the first half, and the higher and livelier second half, which makes the lyrical expression there more intense and more urgent. The fact that bars 1 and 3 lack upbeats gives added emphasis to the important words "wae" and "lang" in stanza 1, to the repeated "love" in stanza 2, and to the longing "O" in stanza 3. But the song is not one of Burns's best. Its somewhat rhetorical style ("Love, thou hast pleasures, and deep hae I loved; / Love thou hast sorrows, and sair hae I proved") and the name "Phillis" give it a tinge of eighteenth-century English poetry, which is not quite in unison with the unpretentiousness of the Scottish tune.

46

A love-song of a more uncomplicated and happy kind is "Young Jockey was the blythest lad" (310). Through the frequent use of repetitions and words with pleasant associations Burns gives this lyric an extrovert character which finely responds to the cheerful expression of the tune. He also takes advantage of the contrast between the two sections of the tune to convey the emotions behind the girl's words. The first four lines of stanza 1 describe the lad in an objective way: "Fu' blythe" the lad whistles and "Fu' lightly" he dances, and as if to imprint this on the listener the word "blythe" is used twice. With the lift in the second half of the tune, its shift from minor to major and its less jerky rhythm, the lyric now speaks of the girl's feelings for the boy, and her face seems to light up at the thought of her own relations to him:

> He roos'd my een sae bonie blue, *praised*
> He roos'd my waist sae genty sma; *gracefully slender*
> And ay my heart came to my mou,
> When ne'er a body heard or saw.

In the second stanza the minor first part of the tune with its energetic, snapped rhythm becomes aptly descriptive of the scene—young Jockey "toils" on the plain through "wind and weet" (*rain*) and through "frost and snaw". In the last half-stanza the lad comes home, he takes the girl in his arms, and the gaiety of the situation is enhanced by the switch to the high register and the major quality of the tune, and the tension of the hard work is released through the smoother rhythm.

One group of Burns's females grow from girlhood to womanhood through the experience of motherhood. A common feature of Scottish life in the eighteenth century which is reflected in the folk-songs, is the young girl who has been seduced and deserted by her lover. Burns picked up this traditional theme and to tunes of both light-hearted and reflective characters he wrote lyrics which mirror different aspects of such situations. He shows deep understanding and sympathy for these girls, and his fine psychological insight into the female mind reveals itself particularly in these songs.

A young and very inexperienced girl is depicted in "To the Weaver's gin ye go" (194), in which the girl's encounter with the erotic side of love comes very abruptly. Her "heart was ance as blythe and free / As simmer days were lang", but innocence met with bitter experience and her singing changed to sighing. There is a foreshadowing of the disastrous event already at the beginning ("But a bonie, westlin weaver lad / Has gart me change my sang" *made*), and although there are elements of delight and joy and excitement in the song there is also a sense of doom hovering over it. The shame and fear of the girl is the underlying sentiment of the song and it is expressed in the last stanza:

47

> But what was said, or what was done,
>   Shame fa' me gin I tell;   *befall; if*
> But Oh! I fear the kintra soon   *country people*
>   Will ken as weel's mysel!   *know*

Her words are sung to the low, monotonous part of the tune, which is centered round one note (F-sharp) and has a descending melodic contour (example 13).

"To the Weaver's gin ye go" (194, <u>SMM</u> No. 103)   Example 13.

My heart was ance as blythe and free As simmer days were lang,

Although it is lively, the tune also strikes a tone of regret and hopelessness through the incessant drumming character of the reiterated F-sharp. This also calls to mind the regular thump of the loom, which accompanies the girl's sighing and sobbing (notice the monotonous effect of the repetition and alliteration in "But the weary, weary warpin o't", *weaving*).

But, as Kinsley points out, the "blend of delight and regret" is also palpable in the chorus because of its "melancholy final phrase". This chorus, which is traditional (*Notes,* p. 24), is a jocular, yet serious comment on the girl's words in the stanzas. What happens if a girl goes to the weaver at night is said only by implication, and the chorus is meant as a warning to other young girls:

> To the weaver's gin ye go, fair maids,   *if*
>   To the weaver's gin ye go,
> I rede you right, gang ne'er at night,   *warn*
>   To the weaver's gin ye go.

As it is not the girl who speaks in it, it becomes the comment of a detached observer and recalls the function of the chorus in a Greek drama. The tune has an assertively rising melodic line in major, before it falls into minor in the last bar, which gives it that curiously sad twist at the end. Alexander Keith aptly describes the significance of this minor end thus: "Sprightly enough through three-quarters of its length, it [the chorus] drops to the minor in the concluding bar, with an odd simulation of warning, a sort of admonitory, cautious finger wagged before the face of the lassie to enforce the prophecy of the dire consequences, 'to the weaver's gin ye go.' "[16]

The girl of "Here's his health in water" (583 A, for a discussion of the musical manuscript of this song, see Ch. 1, n. 28) is in the same predicament.

---

[16] Keith, *Burns and Folk-song,* pp. 25—26.

She is pregnant, deserted, and has to stand "the kintra clatter" (*the country people's gossip*), but she has a less worried and more cheerful attitude than the weaver-lassie. She curses the "wanton sides" and the flattering tongue of the boy, yet with a shrug of the shoulders she gives him the toast:

> Although my back be at the wa',
> And though he be the fautor,   *wrong-doer*
> Although my back be at the wa',
> Yet here's his health in water.—

There is no sadness or regret in this song. The tune is gay and extrovert, and in the first half its melodic lines are mainly falling, except at the end where it emphatically rises one octave and the girl can be imagined lifting her hand for the toast: "Yet here's his health in water" (see ill., Ch. 1). In the second half there is emphasis on "O wae gae by" (*may evil befall*), "Sae brawly's he" (*admirably*) and "Till for his sake" because of the lifts in the tune. This is where the girl reveals that she is angry with the boy, but she quickly resumes her attitude of "never mind" and forgives him.

"The rantin dog the Daddie o't" (80) is also a song in which a young mother tries to grasp her situation with humour. It presents a young girl who enjoys life, love and sex and lets nothing depress her. She has a remedy for all the difficulties she might meet as an unmarried mother, and this is "the rantin dog the daddie o't" (*merry-making*). Her tune is cheerful and her attitude optimistic. She knows much more about life than the girl in "To the Weaver's gin ye go", and she also knows how to meet it with both its hardships and its joys. The young weaver-lassie is filled with fear and shame after her introduction to sex, but this lassie thoroughly enjoys it, in spite of the fact that it puts her on the "creepie-chair" (tree-legged stool, used as a stool of repentance in church). In a very female way she asks for protection ("O Wha my babie-clouts will buy" *babie-linen*) and attention ("O Wha will tent me when I cry" *care for*), and in a frank and open manner she sings out her passion ("Wha will mak me fidgin fain; / Wha will kiss me o'er again" *make me excited*).

The tune of the song consists of two sections (taking one stanza each) which are melodically built up in the same way. The first two-bar phrase of each section, corresponding to one line in the lyric, lies within the F-major triad, the second within the E-flat major, the third again within the F-major, and the fourth, which is exactly the same in both sections, leads on to the end-cadence, which is in F-major. For this air Burns has created a song with a very fine sense of structure and unity. The material he used was partly traditional, partly Ramsay's, and partly his own. A song in David Herd's collection probably gave him the idea of the repeated question-word:

> *O wha* will shoe thy bonny feet?
> *Or wha* will glove thy hand?
> *Or wha* will lace thy middle-jimp?[17]

whereas he owed the metre, the binding-rhyme (aaab/cccb/dddb etc.) and the thematic material to "The Cordial", Ramsay's song set to the same tune in *SMM*:

> What if I shou'd waking *ly*
> When the Hoboys are gawn *by*,
> Will ye tent me when I *cry*,
>   My Dear, I'm faint and iry?

(Quoted by Kinsley)

To the aaab-stanza Burns added the form of the triple question from Herd, so that the three lines are not only united at the end by the same rhyme, but also at the beginning by the same word. Each line is thought-contained, just like the two-bar phrase is self-contained in the triad. Finally, he made the last line a refrain and an answer to the questions, which was an original idea, not suggested by any known material:

> O Wha my babie-clouts will buy,
> O Wha will tent me when I cry;
> Wha will kiss me where I lie,
> The rantin dog the daddie o't.

This corresponds to the musical pattern where the last phrase, common to both sections of the tune, carries the refrain, and the three triad-phrases the questions. Kinsley notes this and points out how well the air "sustains the triple question and the energetic answer of Burns's stanza". This is a beautiful example of the unity of poetry and music which by far excels that of Ramsay's song. The repetitions suggest an urgency in the girl's questions and the nuances in her voice are brought about by the variations provided by the tonal shifts between F and E-flat major and by the change of register between the two halves of the tune.

Just as optimistic in a similar situation is the girl in "Duncan Gray" (204, for the tune, see 394), based on a traditional bawdy song. Although the sexual references of the old song are subtilized, Burns has kept the style and the droll situation. It is particularly because of the laughing refrain (taken from the old song and very expressive on two long emphatic notes) in the first half-stanzas that the song refuses to be serious, and this in spite of the fact that the girl shows indignation with Duncan Gray:

---

[17] Quoted by Otto Ritter, *Quellenstudien zu Robert Burns 1773—1791*, Palaestra 20 (Berlin: Mayer & Müller, 1901), p. 131.

Weary fa' you, Duncan Gray,	*a curse on you*
Ha, ha the girdin o't,	*girthing, copulating*
Wae gae by you, Duncan Gray,	*may evil befall*
Ha, ha the girdin o't;	
When a' the lave gae to their play,	*the rest*
Then I maun sit the lee-lang day,	*must; all day*
And jeeg the cradel wi' my tae	*rock*
And a' for the bad girdin o't.—	

The song has a very gay tune. It is brisk and energetic and has an undotted four-beat rhythm which finely sustains the vigorous language. Because of this cheerful musical dimension and because of the prospect of marriage in the last stanza, there is no tragedy about this song.

A more reflective song is "Bonie Dundee" (157). It has a wider emotional range as it expresses affectionate love towards both lover and child, and it is also the one which is most centred round the theme of mother and child. It expresses an almost holy stillness, yet also the shivering of passionate love. It is the most romantic of the songs in this group, and lyric and tune in conjunction sensitively convey the tenderness of the girl's feelings. The song is partly traditional, but the second stanza is definitely by Burns. There are many versions of the old song, but Kinsley points out that "Burns's fragment is the only one that expresses the feelings of the seduced girl". The first half of the tune (AA) lies low, whereas the second (BC) is intenser in the higher register. It starts high, leaps down an octave but rises again in a very expressive way. On the whole the intervals are dramatically wider in B than in A, which is more evenly undulating. The triple rhythm has a lullaby-quality which finely sustains the tenderness of the lyric and creates an image of the young mother rocking the child in her lap.

The first, traditional, stanza perceptively responds to the difference of expression between the two halves of the tune. The first half-stanza (for the low part of the tune) is an objective presentation of the situation. It introduces the theme of the girl who has been made pregnant by "a young brisk Sodger Laddie", whereas the second half-stanza takes us straight into the emotional life of this girl:

O gin I saw the laddie that gae me't!	*that*
Aft has he doudl'd me upon his knee;	*dandled*
May Heaven protect my bonie Scots laddie,	
And send him safe hame to his babie and me.	

With the intensive lifts in the tune her thoughts seem to wander away to the laddie she is in love with and they merely touch upon the child. On the return to the low part of the tune in the first four lines of the second stanza all her attention now turns to the baby, the music being illustrative of an action almost—from having wistfully looked away, she now looks down at the baby in her lap. To the rocking tune she gives him her blessings: "My blessins upon thy sweet, wee lippie! / My blessins upon thy bonie e'e brie!" (*eye-brow*). The music gives variation to the repeated blessings as the second lies a fifth higher than the first. From "my blessins" she moves to "Thy smiles are sae like my blyth Sodger laddie", which prepares for the switch of attention in the last four lines (for the high part of the tune). Here Burns makes the girl react in the same way as she did in the first stanza: she turns away from the baby again, her thoughts are still centred round it, but they are now also circling round the "dadie dear". They are the proud but affectionate thoughts of a mother, who has great dreams for her son. Best of all he will be like his father and remind her of him. The transition from the low part of the tune to the more dramatic and intense second half is marked in the text by the word "but":

But I'll big a bow'r on yon bonie banks,	*build*
Whare Tay rins wimplin by sae clear;	*runs meandering*
And I'll cleed thee in the tartan sae fine,	*clothe*
And mak thee a man like thy dadie dear.	

Common in sentiment is "I look to the North" (327), which is also about a dreaming girl who wistfully hopes for her lover's return. She also has been left alone with her baby, but her thoughts are less centred round the child. The rocking is more of an accompaniment to her thoughts of her lover. In the first stanza she looks to the north, she looks to the south and she looks to the east. Her thoughts span wide over the "far foreign land" and the "wide rolling sea", but nowhere does she find her lover. The tune lies low, it is undotted and not very exciting. In the second half of the song, however, it lifts an octave, it urgently repeats itself on a rising fifth, and most important, the rhythm changes from equal to dotted quavers. Her eyes now turn towards the west, and "West" is mentioned twice, and her dreams become happier: "For far in the West lives he I lo'e best, / The Man that is dear to my babie and me".

As we have seen the girls in the group of songs discussed in this chapter are full-fledged characters, capable of deep emotions and intelligent thinking. They are caught in various life-situations, acting and feeling, something which makes them and their emotions seem very real. There is a wide range of brisk and extrovert tunes as well as of more reflective ones, and a happy wedding of text and tune brings out the characters of the girls and enhances their emotions. Their language is conversational, the poetic diction limpid and the musical idiom simple. The majority of the girls also come alive through the fact that they speak for themselves in the songs—life is viewed through their eyes and described in their own words.

52

A much more passive and less real kind of woman is presented in the songs of the following chapter, where love and women are seen from the man's point of view. As we shall see these songs are less successful as characterizations of the man or the woman, but they may be very effective in expressing an emotion.

Chapter 4

Love and the Man

> "Whenever I want to be more than ordinary *in song*; to be in some
> degree equal to your diviner airs; do you imagine I fast & pray for the
> celestial emanation?—Tout au contraire! I have a glorious recipe . . . I
> put myself on a regimen of admiring a fine woman; & in proportion
> to the adorability of her charms, in proportion you are delighted with
> my verses.—"
>
> Robert Burns, Letter 644

The other type of woman who emerges from Burns's songs is the idealized
woman as she is seen through men's eyes, and through Burns's eyes when his
style is English, neoclassical and genteel. Many of these songs arose from
Burns's own experience and were written for, or in remembrance of, one particular woman, and, as Crawford points out, such songs are usually inferior to
the more impersonal ones, which do not have a biographical background.[1]
These women are all cast in the same mould, and they are created not to act for
themselves, but to be an object of adoration for the men—"To adore thee is my
duty", says the man in "The bonny wee thing" (357). With a few exceptions
there is very little dramatic action or characterization (of either woman or
man) in these songs. If not purely descriptive, they centre round the man's
feelings towards a woman. They are songs of sentiment and the tunes are, in
the best ones, expressive of the dominant emotion in the poem. Within this
group of love songs there are songs which are pure descriptions of a woman,
songs dealing with the man's feelings, and songs of parting.

Burns's very first poetic attempt was a love song in praise of a young girl,
"O once I lov'd" (1),[2] written when he was only sixteen. In his *Commonplace
Book* Burns wrote the following as an introduction to the song:

There is certainly some connection between Love, and Music & Poetry . . . For my
own part I never had the least thought or inclination of turning Poet till I got once heart-
ily in Love, and then Rhyme & Song were, in a manner, the spontaneous language of

---

[1] Crawford, p. 268.

[2] The tune which Burns prescribed, "I am a man unmarried", was not recovered until quite
recently by Thomas Crawford, who had it in a transcript from George St. J. Bremner whose
father had sung it (*Weekly Scotsman*, March 12, 1965). It was printed for the first time with
Burns's lyric in Robert D. Thornton's *Robert Burns: Selected Poetry and Prose*, pp. 97 and
258.

54

my heart. The following composition was the first of my performances, and done at an early period of life, when my heart glowed with honest warm simplicity; unacquainted, and uncorrupted with the ways of a wicked world. The performance is, indeed, very puerile and silly; but I am always pleased with it, as it recals to my mind those happy days when my heart was yet honest and my tongue was sincere. The subject of it was a young girl who really deserved all the praises I have bestowed on her. (*1CPB*, p. 3)

The song is an immature attempt to marry words to music, yet interesting as it is the first. It is the description of an idealized young lassie, endowed with such assets as virtue, modesty, decency and innocence:

> O once I lov'd a bonnie lass,
>   An' aye I love her still,
> An' whilst that virtue warms my breast
>   I'll love my handsome Nell.
>
> As bonnie lasses I hae seen,
>   And mony full as braw,   *handsome*
> But for a modest gracefu' mein
>   The like I never saw.

Rhythmically the words glide in smoothly with the music, forming the ballad stanza 4-3-4-3, but as yet Burns is not aware of the poet as the interpreter of the expression of the tune. It is significant that his own, rather self-conscious, criticism of the song is exclusively concerned with the poetic merits. The relationship with the music is not touched upon. About the first and second stanzas (quoted above) he says:

The first distic of the first stanza is quite too much in the flimsy strain of our ordinary street ballads; and on the other hand, the second distic is too much in the other extreme. The expression is a little awkward, and the sentiment too serious. Stanza the second I am well pleased with; and I think it conveys a fine idea of that amiable part of the Sex—the agreables; or what in our Scotch dialect we call a sweet sonsy Lass. (*1CPB*, pp. 4—5)

There is a blend of Scottish and English in the song, which mirrors the mixture of the two languages and the two cultures in the Scottish society at that time. What Burns had heard and read were both Scottish folk-songs as they lived among the common people, and English genteel songs as they appeared in eighteenth-century collections like *The Lark* (London, 1740) and *The Charmer* (Edinburgh, 1749). Crawford points out that although "words like 'virtue, reputation, qualities,' or metaphors like 'it's innocence and modesty that polishes the dart,' are from the common stock of art-song, they had in all probability become folk material by the time they reached Burns".[3]

The song about "handsome Nell" has very little sentiment and characterization. It seems a rather conventional description of a girl, attached to a tune

---

[3] Crawford, pp. 2—3.

whose expression is not quite congenial to the poem. With its very strong Scottish flavour (it is pentatonic and its first half is built up round only three notes), it asks for a poem in the folk-song style. Especially when sung with its fal-lal-de-lal-chorus, so strongly connected with the traditional songs, Burns's song seems a bit of a hybrid and not very successful.

A later, more mature, but still very conventional eulogy of a woman is "Beware o' bonie Ann" (288), composed "out of compliment to Miss Ann Masterton, the daughter of my friend Allan Masterton", who wrote the tune (*Notes*, p. 43). The song abounds in stock-expressions such as "Her een sae bright, like stars by night, / Her skin is like the swan", clichés like "The captive bands may chain the hands, / But loove enslaves the man", abstractions such as "Youth, grace and love attendant move, / And pleasure leads the van", and the description of "bonie Ann" does not come alive. The tune is pedestrian and the internal rhymes, emphasized on the long, emphatic notes, make the song stodgy and cumbrous and hardly expressive of the emotions felt for a beautiful young girl.

Even less expressive of either character or emotion is "Lovely Davies" (333). It is a poor performance in the worst of Burns's imitative eighteenth-century English poetic style. Directness and clarity disappear in a cloud of clichés and are muddled by the long and complex tune. Kinsley believes that "Lovely Davies" was what Burns referred to as the "foolish verses, the unfinished production of a random moment, & never meant to have met your ear" (Letter 464); it was sent to Miss Deborah Davies in 1791.

These three songs say little or nothing about the man's feelings for the woman. They are predominantly descriptions of the females, held in a conventional, stylized and sometimes abstract language. As songs they are not very successful, partly because of the lack of simplicity in the poetry and sometimes also in the music, and partly because of the choice of theme: the stylized descriptions lack emotional implications and therefore leave no room for the music to operate. In the next two groups of songs, the stress lies more on the feelings of the man, for a woman in general or in a situation of parting. This type of lyric is better fitted for music, for it suggests an emotion which can be expressed and conveyed also by the tune. The latter either adds a new dimension to the poem or it emphasizes the dominant lyric sentiment.

A fine example of such a song of feeling is "The bonny wee thing" (357), one of Burns's most genuine and delicate expressions of love. Although it has a polished language its import is much more direct than in any other of the songs discussed in this chapter. This is due to its simplicity and to the sensitivity with which the lyric interprets the tune. There is an allusiveness in the text which allows the full emotional gamut of the music to operate. The song conveys a sense of fragility, and implies, as Crawford puts it, "an almost agonised min-

gling of protective tenderness with the conviction of absolute unattainability".[4]
The latest commentator on the song, Cedric Thorpe Davie, calls it "a classic
example of the subtle chemistry that transforms words and music into an entirely new compound".[5] The song is also noted by Alexander Keith who finds
that the "alternation of open and closed vowel sounds, joined with the slurs
and runs of the music, become in some mysterious way full of harmony".[6] As
he says, the song is full of harmony, but the effect is not achieved in "some
mysterious way", as will be shown in the following analysis.

The chorus contains the gist of the song:

> Bonie wee thing, canie wee thing,   *gentle*
> Lovely wee thing, was thou mine;
> I wad wear thee in my bosom,
> Least my Jewel I should tine.—   *loose*

It contains the presentation of the bonie thing as "wee" (repeated three times),
the desire to possess it, the unattainability, the image of the jewel to express the
beauty and smallness of the beloved person, and the fear of losing it. The first
two lines embody the sense of fragility which is the main quality of the song.
Each "wee" is qualified by an adjective, which gives the lines balance and harmony. The change of direction in the melody endows them with different
emotional shades and the music makes the word pregnant with emotion and
meaning. When the first two lines are read there is a tendency to put the stress
on "Bónie wee thing, cánie wee thing, / Lóvely wee thing", whereas the sung
version gives all the emphasis to "wee", the key-word of the song (example 14).

The melody starts high on "bonie" but falls to lean on "wee", it starts high
again on "canie" but then lifts high to rest on "wee", and finally it repeats the
falling pattern of the first phrase for "lovely wee thing". This is a triple pattern
where the second variation is the climax. The repetitions of "wee" are the
balancing points of the first two poetical lines, placed at either end of the
melodic scales, high and low, heavy because they are monosyllabic and

---

[4] Crawford, p. 272.
[5] Thorpe Davie, p. 170.
[6] Keith, *Burns and Folk-song*, p. 24.

emphatic because the notes are long (a crotchet or dotted quavers). The snaps on "bonie" and "canie" in the *SMM* version of the tune lend a kind of gentle shiver to their expression and a hardly noticeable sense of pang in the heart (example 14). This is effected by the lack of upbeats in combination with the energy of the snaps, which accents the plosive consonants in "bonie" and "canie". For the third and fourth lines of the chorus the tune is repeated and the words "wear", "bosom" and "Jewel" are now brought out, and especially "bosom" receives a very warm quality on the top note. Its rounded vowel, *o*, is prolonged through the long note, and the expression of the word is therefore intensified when sung.

The first stanza expresses the innermost wish of the poet and Burns moulds the first line gently on a liquid (*l*), brought out more emphatically by the music, and links the last line with the last of the chorus:

> Wishfu*ll*y I *l*ook and *l*anguish
> In that bonie face o' thine;
> And my heart its stounds wi' anguish,   *thrills*
> Lest my wee thing be na mine.—

This part of the tune does not have the gentle coming and going of the first part, but is much more restless and agitated. The lyric responds to the change in the musical expression very perceptively, for the words, too, imply an emotional agitation. The heart "stounds wi' anguish" and the happiness is of the extreme kind, verging on pain rather than pleasure. The melody has a repetitive pattern and the snaps on the words "heart", "stounds" and "anguish" express the minutest, yet forceful feelings, the pangs of the heart as it were. The second poetical line brightens up, as the tune firmly ascends here after the descents and upsetting skips of the preceding bars. The intense and painful longing in the first line and the sudden overflow of joy in the second at the thought of the beloved face, is something which cannot be conveyed without the music.

The second stanza has balance and harmony in the first line ("Wít, and Gráce, and Lóve, and Béauty"), but is not quite organically connected with the rest of the song. It is more pretentious with the abstractions of the first line, the clichés of the third ("To adore thee is my duty"), and its refined diction, and its sentiment is not in such fine unison with the tune as the first stanza is. It expresses not a feeling, but an abstract thought, something which cannot be conveyed as easily in a musical setting. Notice also the less perfect fitting of words to the tune. In the last line, for example, "o' " clumsily falls on a heavy note.

A subtle fusion of lyric and tune can also be found in "Wilt thou be my Dearie" (444), a song which expresses tender and protective love for a young girl, instead of the fragility and sense of unattainability which is the main quality of "The bonny wee thing". The song is spun round the affectionate word "Dearie" in the first stanza and the wish embodied in "lo'es me" in the second, both repeated four times on the same melodic phrase (the second time as a variation) and both emphatic through the rhythm, low register, and melodic shape of the tune (example 15). "Wilt thou be my Dearie" and "Lassie, say thou lo'es me" are the recurring thoughts of the lover, haunting his mind and intensifying through the repetition. Burns displays a strong sense of structure in this song and the close correspondence between the form of the tune and the form of the poem is important for its emotive impact.

The first phrase (a) of the tune consists of three bars, a_1, a_2 and a_3, where bar a_1 (marked by "x" in the quotation below) is the recurring melodic theme (example 15). It takes the opening question "Wilt thou be my Dearie" and its variation in the first stanza, and in the second, the more entreating "Lassie, say thou lo'es me". This phrase is the prelude to the rest of the song. It is marked off from the subsequent phrases by a double-bar in the musical notation and a colon in the text. It also differs from the rest of the tune in being a three-bar phrase, corresponding to three lines in the poem. The three following phrases, bcc^1, are regular two-bar phrases, which carry the development of the poetical and musical themes introduced in the prelude. The x-theme of the introduction is repeated in the last bar of c and c^1. The thematical structure of the poem follows that of the music, new material being introduced in both b and c, but c^1 being a variation of c through a conversion of word-order:

a	Wilt thou be my Dearie;	x
	When sorrow wrings thy gentle heart,	
	O wilt thou let me chear thee:	x
b	By the treasure of my soul,	
	That's the love I bear thee!	
c	I swear and vow, that only thou	
	Shalt ever be my Dearie—	x
c^1	Only thou, I swear and vow,	
	Shalt ever be my Dearie.—	x

The second stanza has exactly the same structure. The insistent and passionate effect of the beseeching "Wilt thou be my Dearie" and "Lassie, say thou lo'es me" derives partly from the repetition of the musical phrase, partly from the fact that it lies lower and is steadier than the other phrases. These rise high and form the melodic lines on quavers and semi-quaver runs, whereas the x-motif is firmly anchored round the tonic in a steady rhythm and with a syllabic setting. The tonic is a long note (a crotchet) and takes "Dearie" and "lo'es me" (example 15). Thereby these words receive an emotional bearing which is lacking in a read version of the song. The phrase also starts without an upbeat, which is important for the emphasis on "*Wilt* thou" and "*Lassie*".

In the last four lines of each stanza there is a subtle switch of focus, corresponding to the variation in the tune from c to c^1. This is the change from "I

"Wilt thou be my Dearie"
(444, SMM No. 470) Example 15.

Wilt thou be my Dearie;
Lassie say thou lo'es me;

swear and vow, that only thou" to "Only thou, I swear and vow", from the concentration round the lover and his protestation to the more direct address to the beloved. The development is the same in the second stanza, from "Let me, Lassie, quickly die" to the more personal and intimate "Lassie, let me quickly die". The second phrase (c^1) has a more urgent expression because of the unexpected high start without an upbeat, which makes "Only" and "Lassie" the climax and the strongest effusion of overpowering love, although somewhat pathetic in the promise of "Only thou". Kinsley, who has analysed the song, says that it

is a fine example of Burns's best lyrical style—tender, passionate, and direct—and of his skill in wedding music and poetry . . . The low part of the air, the third bar repeating the first, carries the lover's reiterations, plaintive and subdued; and the mood of entreaty is intensified by the lift in the fourth bar. But the song rises to emphatic declaration and impassioned appeal in the higher part, dropping away again into the quieter (but now intensified) final phrases.[7]

Burns himself professed that the tune "is a first-rate favorite of mine, & I have written what I reckon one of my best songs to it" (Letter 620).

Another song of togetherness and tenderness is "O lay thy loof in mine lass" (600). The lyric is set to a beautiful minor tune with a rhythmic lilt which conveys content, peace and security. In the chorus the melodic lines are mainly falling, and the dotted rhythm emphasizes the soft sounds of the liquid *l* and the nasal *m* (see Ch. 2, example 1):

> O *l*ay thy *l*oof in *m*ine *l*ass,   *hand given in pledge*
> In *m*ine *l*ass, in *m*ine *l*ass,
> And swear on thy white hand *l*ass,
> That thou wilt be my ain.

"Mine" is central and embodies the longing, security and warmth of the song. It lies on long notes (crotchets) and is repeated three times, the second on an emphatic leap up (see Ch. 2, example 1). The basic rhythm of the song is dotted, and only when the lyric expresses restlessness and unhappiness does it

---

[7] Also Thorpe Davie has a short analysis of the structure of the tune (p. 173), but he makes no aesthetic judgements.

change into equal notes. This happens in bars 5 and 6, corresponding to the first two lines of each stanza, where also the repeated rise-falls in the melodic curve and the monotonous repetition of the same notes enhance the sense of agitation. When the tune drops into the rocking of the dotted rhythm again, the return is marked in both stanzas by the emphatic "but". At the end of the tune the melody lifts an octave making the last line of each stanza sound more urgent, more direct, and more intimate.

"Louis what reck I by thee" (248) is a fragment of two stanzas in which Burns tells of his love for Jean Amour, his wife. He feels superior to all kings, for he reigns in her heart: "Let her crown my love her law, / And in her breast enthrone me". The song has a touch of melancholy conveyed by the minor mode of the tune, but there is also conviction and strength in the line "Kings and nations, swith awa!" (*quickly away*). Here the tune assertively rises, and at the top of the musical phrase it effectively brings out the exclamation "swith awa!"

"And I'll kiss the yet, yet" (215) likewise expresses content in love. As a lyric, however, it is rather trite and it needs the music to give it its emotional implications:

> When in my arms, wi' a' thy charms,
>   I clasp my countless treasure, O!
> I seek nae mair o' Heav'n to share,
>   Than sic a moment's pleasure, O!
>
> And by thy een sae bony blue,
>   I swear I'm thine forever O!
> And on thy lips I seal my vow,
>   And break it shall I never O!

The song can be found in two versions, one in *SMM* ("And I'll kiss thee yet, yet", 215) and one in *SC* ("Song", 423, for its tune, see 398). The first version (215) consists of the two stanzas quoted above, where each stanza is repeated twice to cover the high part of the tune ("Braes o' Balquhidder"), and the chorus ("An I'll kiss thee yet, yet") is set to the low part. The second version (423) discards the chorus and joins the two stanzas into one, which then forms the second stanza of a new song set to the tune "Cauld kail in Aberdeen". This stanza will be considered here for purposes of comparison although it was not printed in *SMM*. Its first half-stanza (i.e. stanza one of the first set, 215) lies on the low part of the tune and the second on the high. In the second version the two stanzas quoted above are thus united by the tune. They form one organic whole, yet they reveal a difference of expression within its framework as the second half is more intense on the high part of the tune. In the first version, on the other hand, there is no such connection between the two stanzas. The chorus is the wedge between them, and in addition to that, each stanza is tediously repeated twice to cover the tune. The different accentuation of the words, effected by the respective tunes, also affects the expression of the two songs. In the first version (215) there is a leap of an octave in bar 5 which gives an unnecessarily strong accent to the words "charms", "share", "blue", and "vow". In the second version (423) these words lie at the lowest points of the musical phrases, leading the lyrical line more gently and naturally on to the conclusion of the sentence in the following lines.

By comparison the second version appears the better. It gives the lyric a stronger sense of unity and an emotional dimension lacking in the *SMM* version. There is no development in the lyric, no change of emotional gear, and the two stanzas could easily be interchanged. It is therefore very important that the tune, as in the second version, varies the expression between the two. The first four lines will then serve as an introduction to the last four, where the lover gets more involved in the amorous thoughts of the woman and his feelings become more intense.

"The seventh of November" (231) is a less successful expression of happy love. The poetic style seems too pretentious for the brisk and cheerful tune, and Burns has not quite managed to capture its sentiment. The song is a recollection of the "blissful day we twa did meet" and the tune was written by Robert Riddell for the anniversary of his wedding (Letter 271). Possibly the knowledge of this constrained Burns in his choice of theme and prevented him from writing a more light-hearted and humorous lyric. In his comment on this song Dick points out that "Burns was generally and generously wrong when he adopted the melodies of his personal friends",[8] and it seems that he was more successful with the simple, traditional tunes.

"The blue-eyed Lassie" (232) is also set to a tune by Riddell. It describes the "stound, the deadly wound" (*pang*) that came from the "een sae bonie blue" of the lassie and is a rather strained composition. The portrait of the girl is conventional ("Her lips like roses, wat wi' dew, / Her heaving bosom, lily-white"), the repetitions laboured and the internal rhymes pathetic ("She talk'd, she smil'd, my heart she wyl'd", "But spare to speak, and spare to speed" wyl'd *beguiled*). The first stanza seems more inspired than the second, however, and it does not have the internal rhymes, nor the repetitions. The tune is unsingable for the average singer because of its wide range and unfit for textual setting because of its over-elaboration.

In "O, were I on Parnassus Hill" (228) the poet asks the Muse to inspire his lay "That I might catch poetic skill, / To sing how dear I love thee". It is a positive effusion of love in a simple and unpretentious style, but set to a tune ("My love is lost to me") which gives it a touch of melancholy. This chimes ill

---

[8] Dick, *The Songs*, p. 364.

with the theme, for there are no verbal implications of sadness. It seems that Burns was not very particular about the tune for this poem, or that he realized that it needed a gayer one, for he suggested "Dainty Davie" as an alternative to Thomson (Letter 580), a major and much lighter tune than "My love is lost to me".

"She's fair and fause &c." (385) mirrors another view on love and women, namely that of the woman as capricious ("A woman has't by kind"). Her role in man's life is that of a passing joy and a passing grief ("But woman is but warld's gear, / Sae let the bonie lass gang", *world's property*). This has its musical counterpart in the blend of major and minor in the tune. The song lacks organic unity, however. As Kinsley points out it is stylistically a hybrid, lines 1—8 being in the Scots tradition and lines 9—16 being reminiscent of English lyrics. As a merit mention should be made of Burns's fine use of the emphatic upward leap in the second half of the tune. In the first stanza this is where description is replaced by action and in the second, advice by dramatic outcry ("O woman, lovely woman fair!").

In the following songs the protagonists are young boys and not mature men. The themes and the simplicity of style (the songs are very much in the folk style) indicate a more unpretentious kind of love than in the songs discussed above where the protective and gentle passion dominated. "Eppie McNab" (355) is about disappointment in love and shows Burns's skill at developing the structure and refining the expression of a traditional song. His model was a bawdy song later printed in *The Giblet Pye* (c. 1806) or, as Kinsley suggests, a variant of it. The first stanza of that song is the dialogue which Burns has used as the first stanza of his own. He has, however, developed the dialogue-form in a very intricate way to express the feelings of the deceived lover on the one hand and the dramatic situation on the other.

The tune is long. It consists of two sections of two parts each, where the first section carries the dialogue:

> O saw ye my dearie, my Eppie M^{c}nab?
> O saw ye my dearie, my Eppie M^{c}nab?
> She's down in the yard, she's kissin the Laird,
> She winna come hame to her ain Jock Rab.—

The repeated question, slightly varied through the music, and the descending phrases of the melody express the sadness of the wondering boy. The answer is given on the high, ascending part of the first section of the tune and its climax on the top note in bar 13 dramatically brings out the word "winna", as if to emphasize the fact that the girl has changed her mind. The boy's reaction to the girl's faithlessness is strong and he needs a full stanza to ponder over it. He is prepared to forgive and beseeches the girl to come back:

> O come thy ways to me, my Eppie M^{c}nab;
> O come thy ways to me, my Eppie M^{c}nab;
> What-e'er thou has done, be it late, be it soon,
> Thou's welcome again to thy ain Jock Rab.—

For the entreating first line the tune rises and falls in minor, and for the second (with the same words) the same melodic figure is repeated, but this time in major. This suggests a development from pessimism to optimism which leads up to the hopeful and all-forgiving last two lines.

The last two stanzas have the same pattern of question and answer for the first section of the tune and a monologue for the second, but the situation is much more dramatic here. The repeated question is full of hope and expectancy ("What says she, my dearie, my Eppie M^{c}nab?"), but the answer is harsh and bitter and the contrast is displayed against the change of direction (from falling to rising phrases) in the tune: "She lets thee to wit, that she has thee forgot, / And for ever disowns thee, her ain Jock Rab." The last stanza expresses disappointment and despair with the sighing rise-falls in the tune to reinforce it. Willingness to forgive has now been replaced by anger and regret.

The dramatic effect in the song is heightened by the way in which Burns has set the two parts of the dialogue to alternating sections of the tune. In the first and third stanzas the boy turns to the other person who is the link between him and Eppie. In the second and fourth, he turns away from him, and his thoughts are instead directed towards Eppie. In this way the sung version brings out the contrasts much more effectively than when the poem is read out loud.

"Tibbie Dunbar" (285) is about a young laddie's love for a sweet young lassie called Tibbie Dunbar. Free from pretentiousness and in an honest and conversational manner this song spins round the old theme of love and money. It is light-hearted and straightforward and with its simple diction and brisk, energetic tune it has the sparkling freshness which is the characteristic of Burns's best songs in the folk-style. The lover's repeated invitation is common in Scottish folk-poetry and in this song Burns has used it very cleverly to express the urgency of the boy's request:

> O wilt thou go wi' me, sweet Tibbie Dunbar;
> O wilt thou go wi' me, sweet Tibbie Dunbar:
> Wilt thou ride on a horse, or be drawn in a car,
> Or walk by my side, O sweet Tibbie Dunbar.—

As the musical phrases for the first two lines are slightly different, the expression of the identical questions is varied. The second time the lover lowers his voice at the cadence and becomes more passionate, as it were. The stress lies on "wilt" as it falls on the first beat of the bar ("O wĭlt") and this is also the central word for the boy in his opening question. In the third line he tries to make his invitation more attractive. He specifies it and the tune changes into a cheerful dotted swing. The stress is now on "ride" and "drawn" as "Wilt thou" falls on the upbeat. "Wilt" also has a shorter note-value than in the first two lines (example 16).

"Tibbie Dunbar" (285, SMM No. 207)   Example 16.

O wilt thou go wi' me, sweet Tibbie Dunbar;

O wilt thou go wi' me, sweet Tibbie Dunbar:

Wilt thou ride on a horse, or be drawn in a car,

Once the initial advances are over, the boy gets braver and more excited and he makes his declaration of love, honest and untempted by riches:

> I care na thy daddie, his lands and his money;
> I care na thy kind, sae high and sae lordly: *kindred*
> But say thou wilt hae me for better for waur,   *worse*
> And come in thy coatie, sweet Tibbie Dunbar.—

Here the tune rises emphatically and there is energy and urgency in the boy's proposal. Especially expressive of his infatuated impatience is the repeated "care" on the energetic repeated upward leap. The fact that the word falls on a dotted note increases its emphasis. If the boy was modest in his proposal in the first verse and centred round Tibbie (he repeats her name three times), he is now indignant at the circumstances under which he has to make the proposal, and he summons up all his energy to convince the girl that he loves her for her own sake and not for her money. After the excitement in the first two lines the tune gradually drops and becomes more intimate. It falls back into the cadence of the first half and the boy again mentions the name of his "sweet Tibbie Dunbar".

In the early "Song" (6) another Tibbie is addressed. The conflict between love and money is much more outspoken here, and also the girl's response is part of the song. She has despised the boy because of his lack of money. But like the boy in the later song, he strongly protests that he does not want to marry for money, and if she does not want him she can go. He is proud and has a self-confidence which is expressed in words as well as in music. Both the chorus (quoted below) and the refrain-line in each stanza with their energetic snaps are particularly expressive of the boy's indignation. When confronted with the haughty young lassie he gets angry and one can imagine him demonstratively turning his back on her:

> Tibby I hae seen the day
> Ye wadna been sae shy
> For laik o' gear ye lightly me   *lack of money; scorn*
> But trowth I care na by—

The dotted two-beat rhythm of the tune has a sense of stability which emphasizes the boy's uncompromising character. The words are short (Ritter thinks that the song has something eruptive about it because of the one-syllable words),[9] and the setting is syllabic, which gives it a conversational character. The rhymes of the stanzas all end on closed syllables which, with the Scottish "clipped" consonants,[10] add to its decisive and assertive expression. The song is very long and lacks the conciseness of "Tibbie Dunbar", but as an early attempt it is interesting, since it shows an awareness of the latent expression of a tune.

Songs of love are often songs of parting with Burns and one of his most famous in this genre is the "Song" (337) beginning "Ae fond kiss, and then we sever". This and "Gloomy December" (336) were sent to Clarinda, the married woman with whom Burns had an intense, but platonic love-relationship, before she was to sail to Jamaica to meet her husband, and both express the sadness of the poet before the parting. Of the two, "Gloomy December" is painted in the darker colours in both words and music. The key to its emotional pitch lies in the lines "Sad was the parting thou makes me remember, / Parting wi' Nancy, Oh, ne'er to meet mair!", repeated in the last stanza as the thought recurring in the poet's mind. There reigns a sense of absolute hopelessness in the song. The setting is dark and gloomy, it is winter and the landscape is bare. As Crawford points out, the stormy weather is symbolic of the tempests within the poet,[11] the leaves of the summer are gone, like the "last hope and last comfort" in his heart. Words of distress and unhappiness preponderate, like "gloomy", "sorrow and care", "sad" and "dire".

The sadness and anguish of the song lie also in the tune, which is heavy and sighing. The slow tempo, the triple rhythm, the repeated terraced descents, the high starts without upbeats and the minor mode (Aeolian)—all these aspects are conducive to an expression of gloom. The accent falls heavily on the first

---

[9] Ritter, p. 7.

[10] This is an impressionistic term sometimes used for the slightly glottalized and aspirated consonants at the end of a word.

[11] Crawford, p. 332.

beat of each falling figure, mainly because there is no upbeat and the melodic line is descending, but also because of the triple rhythm, which does not give a secondary stress in the bar (example 17). Through this pattern the key-words are emphasized in a much stronger way than if the poem is only read. Furthermore the tempo of the song is much slower than a read version can ever be.

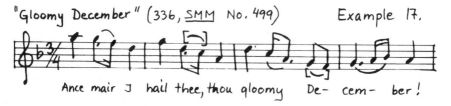

"Gloomy December" (336, SMM No. 499)   Example 17.

Ance mair J hail thee, thou gloomy De- cem- ber!

Notice for instance the effective prolonged dark vowel in "gloomy". There is a monotony in the repeated falling phrases (the form is AABA) which is broken only by the change of melodic direction in B. Here the phrase starts low, rises and stays high in four bars. This intensifies the positive note struck in lines 5—6 of the first stanza: "Fond lovers' parting is sweet, painful pleasure, / Hope beaming mild on the soft parting hour". The second half of the second stanza ties up with the introductory lines of the song, "indicating a cyclical development within the song—a return to the starting-point" as Crawford puts it.[12] It is only varied a little in the wording, "still" emphasizing the unchangingness of the spiritual gloom, and the rise in B making it even more painful before the return to the despondency of A:

B Still as I hail thee, thou gloomy December,
   Still shall I hail thee wi' sorrow and care;
A For sad was the parting thou makes me remember,
   Parting wi' Nancy, Oh, ne'er to meet mair.—

The mannered diction may strike an unsincere note, but the poem is wedded to a very expressive tune in such a masterly way that, as a unified composition of text and tune, it has a genuine and deep dimension of sadness and sorrow.

 The second song written on the same occasion is a much less gloomy creation. The total despair is gone and although there are lines like "Dark despair around benights me" and "Warring sighs and groans I'll wage thee", the tune speaks another language. The time is lighter (6/8 instead of 3/4), the melodic contour more positive with its rising phrases, and the mode is now major (Ionian). There is a coming and going in the rising and falling phrases which is suggestive of rocking or of peaceful sighing, and the light and tender lilt of the beautiful tune seems to point to an acceptance of the parting. As an

---

[12] Crawford, p. 332.

afterthought the first stanza is repeated at the end, but then to be sung to the high section of the tune as if the words have received a new and more intense meaning:

> Ae fond kiss, and then we sever!
> Ae fareweel, Alas, for ever!
> Deep in heart-wrung tears I'll pledge thee,
> Warring sighs and groans I'll wage thee.—

"Sae far awa" (572) is very much in the same mood and this song also is assumed to refer to Burns's parting with Clarinda. It is a rather conventional poem about the parting of two lovers set to a tune of beautiful lyric implications. With its undulating phrases and its major quality with a minor close it has a wide emotional range. It gives the lyric a dimension of bitter-sweet sadness which the words by themselves fail to convey. Throughout the song echoes the recurring thought of the lover's mind, "sae far awa", expressively falling on the repeated falling cadence (bars 4, 8, 12 and 16).

"The Northern Lass" (123) is a more concentrated song, centring round the theme of the emotional inseparability of two lovers:

> Though cruel Fate should bid us part,
>   Far as the Pole and Line,
> Her dear idea round my heart
>   Should tenderly entwine:
>
> Though mountains rise, and desarts howl,
>   And oceans roar between;
> Yet dearer than my deathless soul
>   I still would love my Jean.—

The tune has a large range, with as wide a span as the words have. The two stanzas are structured similarly ("Though"—"Her dear", "Though"—"Yet dearer"), but the second is more dramatic. Here the tune starts high, there is an increase of quavers and the lover's promises are more excited. Burns now uses three images and three verbs in the first two lines to demonstrate the depth of his love, whereas in the first there is only one.

In "My bony Mary" (242) the parting is seen in much lighter colours. Four lines from an old song (*Notes*, p. 45) set the tone of the song. They are simple and coupled by Burns to a major tune with optimistically rising phrases:

> Go fetch to me a pint o' wine,
>   And fill it in a silver tassie;
> That I may drink, before I go,
>   A service to my bonie lassie:

To this he adds, for the second half of the tune, a description of the rocking boat and the blowing wind, which reminds the protagonist that he must leave his "bony Mary". These lines describe the background scenery and are not thematically linked with the old lines, yet the tune and the simple diction make one organic whole of the two halves. The second stanza is much more pompous with a theme of war which does not quite grow out of that in the first stanza. But by returning to the theme of the sea in the last four lines Burns connects it with the opening of the poem. This return falls on the lift in the second half of the tune, which intensifies the switch from the description of heroic war to the more personal feelings of the protagonist in the moment of parting.

In "Fair Eliza" (370) the theme of parting is linked with that of the despised lover. With its clichés and sentimental diction the song gives a rather flat impression when read. The dramatic qualities and the variation of the emotional pitch have to be looked for in the relation between the lyric and the tune. The song is very interesting as it is printed with two different tunes in *SMM*, both of which Burns had suggested as suitable for his poem. He originally wrote the poem for the air No. 112 in Patrick McDonald's *Collection of Highland Vocal Airs* (printed in Edinburgh, ca. 1784), but at an early stage he said to Johnson that No. 113 in the same collection "with a trifling alteration will do charmingly" (Hastie MS, f. 91), and he proposes the following changes:

The alterations are; in the fourth bar of the first & third strains, which are to be the tune, instead of the crotchet, C, & the quavers, G, & E, at the beginning of the bar, make an entire Minim on E, I mean E, the lowest line; take likewise the 5th, 6th & 7th bars of the 2d strain, which is the strain I mean to leave out, & place them instead of the 5th, 6th & 7th bars of the 1st strain, which I . . . (Hastie MS, f. 91)

The two tunes are fairly similar in structure, rhythm and expression, yet the small differences which exist between them completely change the emotive import of the song.

The form of Burns's first choice of tune, printed as No. 367 in *SMM*, is AA^{1}BC, where A consists of two repeated two-bar phrases. As the same theme is then repeated four times and as it is built up round only three notes of a pentatonic scale, its expression is extremely monotonous (example 18). The form of the second tune, printed as No. 368 in *SMM*, is ABCB, which provides for more variation. The melodic change in the first half of the tune (AB instead of AA^1) also corresponds better with the progression in the poem (example 19). The thought in the first two lines is carried on in the third and fourth, and a repetition of tonal material, as in *SMM* No. 367, has an effect which counteracts the development in the poem:

> Turn again, thou fair Eliza,
>   Ae kind blink before we part;
> Rew on thy despairing Lover,
>   Canst thou break his faithfu' heart!

"Fair Eliza" (370, SMM No. 367)   Example 18.

Turn again, thou fair E- li- za, Ae kind blink before we part;

Rew on thy despairing Lover, Canst thou break his faithfu' heart!

"Fair Eliza" (370, SMM No. 368)   Example 19.

Turn a-gain, thou fair E- li- za, Ae kind blink be-fore we part;

Rew on thy des-pairing Lover, Canst thou break his faithfu' heart!

Furthermore the scale of the second version is heptatonic (the Aeolian mode) and it therefore has greater possibilities of tonal variation. It also has a much more active melodic curve and a greater range. In each phrase it ascends almost by an octave before leaping down again, whereas in the first version the phrases are arched within the three-note range. The second version is therefore more dramatic at the beginning and it conveys an active emotion, whereas the first expresses total resignation. Notice especially how the accentuation in the fourth line differs between the two versions. In the first the same phrase is monotonously repeated (with only a very slight variation), giving an emphasis to "break", but yet suggesting acceptance because of the tonal pattern (the arched melodic contour, example 18). In the second version, on the other hand, it is "canst" which is very strongly accented. It falls at the peak of the melodic curve which lies one octave above the tonal (example 19). It is the despairing question-word which is brought out in this version and the implications are therefore different—the lover in the second setting is more desperate and less inclined to give in.

However, in the second half of both versions the tune lies higher and especially in the first stanza this is very effective as the fifth line is a repetition of the first, "Turn again, thou fair Eliza". This is the second attempt of the lover to get his mistress back, and he is now entreating her more intensely: if nothing else is possible, at least pity can be shown. Here the first version is more dramatic than the second as it stays longer in the higher register and allows the word "pity" to be effectively accented on a top-note. By comparison the first version has a much more monotonous and resigned opening than the second, but on the other hand it displays stronger contrasts between the two sections of the tune, suggesting a development from acceptance and resignation to active despair.

In the second stanza the theme is developed, but not lifted up to a higher dramatic pitch. It closes with an echo of the opening lines of the first stanza ("Turn again, thou lovely maiden, / Ae sweet smile on me bestow") as a reinforcement of the thought which is uppermost in the poet's mind. Poetically and structurally the song would have gained from ending here. Framed by a repeated theme ("Turn again" etc.) there lie the conflict, the beseeching, and the despair of the lover. The first two stanzas are directed to the beloved woman, the "fair Eliza". The last stanza, on the other hand, is no longer addressed to her directly. It is rhetorical and its character is completely different from the other two. It rather belongs to a love-song of a happier kind, being a eulogy to the beloved, and giving no hint of unrequited love or despondency. It is therefore ill suited to the melancholy theme of the tune and not organically connected with the rest of the song.

With some exceptions the songs of this chapter differ in poetic style from those of Chapter 3. They also differ in that they are mostly songs of sentiment, where the tunes serve to enhance these sentiments, and never songs of action or character. In the songs of Chapter 3 Burns drew on a tradition which was based on life as it appeared among the common people and in their songs, whereas in many of the songs in this chapter he was influenced by a literary tradition, created in the minds of the poets rather than taken from real life. In the case of the folk-songs Burns managed to stand apart from his sources and use them in his own individual way; he recreated from the material he had found. He was much less successful when indebted to the English eighteenth-century poets. Accordingly many of the songs in this genre seem stereotyped and have an air of imitation and pretentious elegance rather than free creation.

In the next chapter we shall return to the songs which were based on the Scottish tradition and see what Burns could make of both man and woman in the marriage songs. Here again the stress lies on action and on characterization (or caricature) and there is also a great deal of humour.

Chapter 5

Love and Marriage

Domestic and married life was a common theme in the traditional songs, and as Gavin Greig has pointed out, the *dramatis personae* in these songs, husband and wife, are usually depicted with humour, and a humour which sometimes tends to be very broad. Instances of happy relations are rare and the "expression of wedded love is hardly to be looked for when we consider how reticent the northern man is when matters of feeling are involved".[1] Such is also the case with Burns's songs of marriage (which are many of them based on traditional material) and only one, "John Anderson my Jo", is a song of sentiment and the epitomy of a life-long love. In the other songs the scenes and sentiments are comic, or tragi-comic, and the portraits of the men and the women are vivid, sometimes verging on caricature. A recurring theme in these songs is that of the *senex amans,* a young girl unhappily married to an old man. As Kinsley points out (p. 1269), this is an old theme, which is to be found even in medieval literature, but which also survives in many Scottish folk-songs. The present chapter will show how Burns could depict such an ill-mixed liaison from a humorous point of view by exaggerating the abominable character of the man. But the situation may also be the reverse and the man's complaint of his bitchy old wife be the focus of attention in the song, this also an old motif. There are also two songs which deal with life-long marriages, one which takes up the old theme of the impotence of the aging man and his wife's reproaches, and the other which expresses tenderness in old age. In these interpretations of old motifs we find some of the happiest instances in Burns's production of humour, dramatic action, vivid characterization or caricature, and conversational language, all aspects in perfect unison with the form and expression of the tunes.

As has been shown in Chapter 3, Burns had an eye for portraying self-confident and independent young girls. Two such girls will be discussed in the present chapter, as they are to be found within the bounds of wedlock, trying to break loose from an unhappy union. Both songs lay their stress on the description of the man, rather than on the girl's indignation, but through this description and through the music also her character and her feelings are revealed. Temperamental and brimming over with impatience with her old man is Jenny

[1] Greig, *Folk-song in Buchan and Folk-song of the North-east,* pp. 29—30.

of "What can a young lassie do wi' an auld man" (347). Her situation seems rather hopeless at the beginning to judge from the way she repeats the opening, almost rhetorical questions: "What can a young lassie, what shall a young lassie, / What can a young lassie do wi' an auld man?" The repetitions are of course the conventional formula of the folk-song, but the way they are coupled to the tune, and in the context of the whole song, they become indicative of the girl's predicament and of her feelings. There is a tone of despair in her voice which cannot be heard without the music, for it lies primarily in the Aeolian (minor) mode of the tune. What is said by implication is that a young girl, once she is married, is oppressed and cannot decide over her situation. Her only chance is to be really nasty to the man, to "cross him, and wrack him" (*torment*) until he is heartbroken.

"What can a young lassie do wi' an auld man"
(347, SMM No. 316)   Example 20.

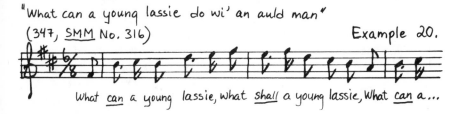

What can a young lassie, what shall a young lassie, What can a ...

The verbs fall heavy on the dotted first beats of the bar, "shall" being more intense as it lies higher. This part of the tune (A) has an energetic, but relaxed swing in the 6/8-time and a decisiveness in the melodic lines, which precludes an expression of passivity and perplexity on the girl's part (example 20). In fact, she proves to be furious in her indignation, and with a terrific suppressed anger she swears over her match-making mother who was tempted to sell her daughter "for siller and lan'". This happens in the second half of the tune (B), which has much more tension than the first. It lies low, but rises progressively on rhythmic snaps and by small intervallic steps (on the notes which form a pentatonic scale, see example 21). Only in the last two bars is there relief from the tension, which the snaps in particular create, when the tune resolves in the dotted swing of the first half. With the force needed to pronounce the consonants falling on the snaps, and with the very marked rhythm which they create, this part of the tune has an almost pictorial effect of the young girl, stamping her foot with impatience, indignation and irritation. But the rhythmic and melodic structure of the second half of the tune also has an emotive import: the sense of the accumulated but suppressed displeasure, the growing agitation (the girl seems to work herself up to an emotional pitch on those repeated ascents), and the relief of tension in the last two bars.

The two following stanzas give a vivid portrait of the horrible old man, and the girl's disgust with him is released. With full armoury she lets fly at him:

A	He's always compleenin frae mornin to e'enin,	
	He hosts and he hirpls the weary day lang:	*cough; limp*
B	He's doyl't and he's dozin, his blude it is frozen,	*stupid; impotent*
	O, dreary's the night wi' a crazy auld man!	

A	He hums and he hankers, he frets and he cankers,	*mumble; loiter;*
	I never can please him, do a' that I can;	*become peevish*
B	He's peevish, and jealous of a' the young fallows,	
	O, dool on the day I met wi' an auld man!	*sorrow*

As both stanzas have a similar structure with the repeated "he", a read version of the song can hardly convey the range of emotion and temperament which lies behind the surface structure. It is particularly the girl's wavering between an outgoing expression of disgust in the first half-stanzas (A) and the inwardly directed, more forceful anger in the second half (B) that cannot be conveyed without the tune. After a general complaint in the first half-stanzas (on the dotted swing in the high register) the girl changes emotional gear and musters up all her anger (for the low, "snapped" section). She gets more and more excited before her emotions subside in the last lines (on the swing and rise of the last two bars), and with an impatient sigh she exclaims: "O, *dreary*'s the night" etc. and "O, *dool* on the day" etc. "Dreary" and "dool" are much more strongly emphasized when sung, as they fall on the peak of a rising melodic phrase.

Through the dotted rhythm the music also reinforces the effective alliterations in lines 6 and 9, which are so expressive of the girl's irritation and disgust. The *h* both imitates the sounds made by the old man himself when "he *h*osts and he *h*irpls" as well as expresses the girl's disgust with him. Her impatience is also effectively brought forth through the plosive *d* in line 7, alliterations which are now accented by the snaps (example 21). This *d* is also to be found in the "O, *d*reary's" and "O, *d*ool" of lines 8 and 12. With the repeated pronoun "he", the alliterations, the onomatopoeic words (see particularly line 9), and the high frequency of verbs, these two stanzas have an accumulative effect. Helped by the tightening of tension in the second half of the tune, they build up and prepare for the climax in the last stanza.

74

Here the girl proves to be cunning. Realizing that she never can please the old man whatever she does, and disappointed enough to be able to carry it through, she follows her auntie's advice: "I'll *cr*oss him, and *wr*ack him untill I hea*rtbr*eak him". Again the collected impact of the apt alliterations (*r* having a rough and forceful effect), the choice of verbs, and the low register of the tune is used to express anger and threat. However, the song has a humorous and happy ending. Relieved at the thought of getting rid of the spiteful man, the girl falls into the swinging lilt of the last two bars, and maybe she dances away while singing "And then his auld brass will buy me a new pan".

Similar in the delineation of the old man, but with more stress on his money and land and much less dependent on the music for its expression is "To daunton me" (209).[2] This song is more straightforward and does not give so many fine psychological shades, humorous touches and emotional overtones as "What can a young lassie". It has no streak of despair but opens with three striking images which call up the picture of a headstrong young girl who is prepared at all costs to withstand the old man she has been wedded to:

> The blude-red rose at Yule may blaw,
> The simmer lilies bloom in snaw,
> The frost may freeze the deepest sea,
> But an auld man shall never daunton me.—

The second stanza presents the man with "his fause heart and his flattering tongue" and again confronts us with the self-willed girl: to be subdued by an old man "is the thing you shall never see". But apart from the man's disgusting appearance, which is also vividly described in stanza 5, it is also the enumeration of goods and material wealth which evokes the girl's loathing for the man, and the accumulative structure of stanzas 3 and 4 emphasizes this. It is the old conflict between love and money which lies in the background, and the girl will not be bought for money:

> For a' his meal and a' his maut,
> For a' his fresh beef and his saut,
> For a' his gold and white monie,
> An auld man shall never daunton me.—

---

[2] H-H (III, pp. 327—28) suggest that Burns probably had his immediate model in a Jacobite song with the following chorus:

> To daunton me, and I so young,
> To daunton me it would be too soon!
> Contrary to him still I'll be,
> And an old Carl shall ne'er daunton me!

Although Burns's song does not explicitly say that the girl is married to the man, I have grouped it with the marriage-songs for two reasons: (1) In Burns's model the girl is married to "an old man neither loving nor kind" (H-H, III, p. 327); (2) With its stress on the description of the man, rather than on the girl's feelings, it is near in expression to "What can a young lassie".

75

The regular four-beat rhythm of the tune and the major mode strengthens the effect of the girl's confidence and the purposefulness of her vow not to be subdued by the old man. She is never at a loss what to do, and she sums it up in the refrain: "For an auld man shall never daunton me". Due to the melodic rises in the tune there is an intensification in each stanza which reaches its climax in bar 9 (taking line 3 of the stanzas). Through this ascent the conclusion in the refrain seems logical: the more the girl thinks of the old man and his offers, the more she is filled with detestation and the more she is convinced that an old man shall never subdue her.

The chorus recapitulates her strong vow in a short and effectful way: "To daunton me, to daunton me, / An auld man shall never daunton me." Burns comments on this chorus in a letter laid into his copy of *CPC* where he makes it clear how he wanted the song to be arranged: "The chorus is set to the first part of the tune [in *CPC*], which just suits it, when *once* play'd or sung over" (Letter 111).[3] The impact of the chorus rests on the resultant conciseness, which emphasizes the contrast between the first two bars (for line 1), descending, low in register, and only preparatory, and the last two bars (for line 2), descending but high and making the girl's purpose sound convincing. But the song does not develop or lead up to a climax, and the stanzas are more or less interchangeable: they all describe the man and his goods and express the underlying contempt felt by the girl.

In "Had I the wyte she bade me" (559, *blame*) an illmatched marriage and its consequences is seen from an outsider's point of view, namely from that of the woman's lover. The woman is practising an old trick, first calling the man a coward for not daring to enter her house, then trying to make him feel sorry for her, as she has such a "ramgunshoch, glum Goodman" (*illtempered*). And with success she lures him over on her side:

I dighted ay her een sae blue,	*wiped*
And bann'd the cruel randy;	*rough fellow*
And weel I wat her willin mou	*well I know*
Was e'en like succarcandie.	

We get only short glimpses of the actual relation between husband and wife in this song, but instead it mirrors the consequences of brutal male treatment as well as gives us another example of the self-confident, emancipated Scottish woman. It is the woman who takes the initiative in the song and she does it very uncompromisingly: "Sae craftilie she took me ben, / And bade me mak

[3] The first part of the tune is repeated in *CPC*, which is the reason why Burns is anxious to say that it should be played only once. This is not how the song is arranged in *SMM*, however. There the first part of the tune in *CPC* takes the stanzas and the second part the chorus, which is not the chorus that Burns prescribed in his letter, but 11. 7—10. Kinsley has arranged the song as Burns wanted it and he prints the tune from *CPC*.

76

nae clatter" (*indoors; uproar*). The tune alters between two major triads and has an assuredness in the dotted four-beat rhythm which effectively supports the quick action and the vigorous language.

But the roles may also be reversed. In other songs it is the man who suffers from being married to a bitchy woman. Not having realized this when he married, for then she was nice and sweet and obedient, he curses the day he brought her into his home and secretly wishes to see her dead. Such is the marital drama as it is exposed in "Whistle o'er the lave o't" (235). Through infinitely small means this song displays the conflict in the man's mind between expectations and reality, his disappointment, and the need to conceal his secret thoughts. Its strong import lies in the tension between the simplicity and tight structure of the tune on the one hand, and the implications and antitheses of the poem on the other. In each stanza there is a relief of tension in what Kinsley calls the "half-jocular abandon of the refrain".

The musical material is limited to five notes and the tune is very short, consisting of only four plus four bars (A + B). A_4 and B_4 are identical (this is the phrase on which the refrain lies), A_1 and A_3 are the same and so are also A_2 and B_2 (for A, see example 22). Each stanza is held together by the binding-rhyme (aaab/cccb etc.) and all the four stanzas by the refrain. The rhythm is dotted or snapped (effective for words like "Maggy", "married", "Whistle" and "maggots"), the setting is syllabic and the expression of strength in the song rests also on the trochaic metre (no upbeats in the music). In this it may be compared with the song set to the same tune in the "Love and Liberty—A Cantata" (84:129), which is more cheerful and carefree and significantly keeps the upbeats and the looser and lighter iambic metre.

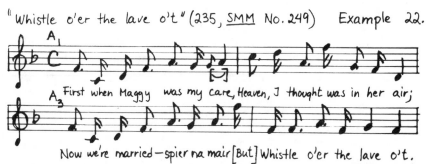

"Whistle o'er the lave o't" (235, SMM No. 249)   Example 22.

First when Maggy was my care, Heaven, I thought was in her air;

Now we're married—spier na mair [But] Whistle o'er the lave o't.

The gist of the song lies in the first stanza with the contrast between then and now, between the heaven of infatuation and the hell of marriage:

> *First* when Maggy was my care,
> Heaven, I thought, was in her air;
> *Now* we're married—spier nae mair—   ask
> Whistle o'er the lave o't.—   rest

Kinsley points out how the word "care" in this stanza has "an ambiguity which sets the tone of the song. She was at first his sweetheart . . . and is now a trouble". The rhetorical antithesis between then and now is emphasized through its collocation on identical musical phrases (A_1 and A_3). They are separated by the second verse line, which is the man's ironic remark on his own mistake. As this line lies in a higher register it also functions as a musical contrast. The strong effect of the juxtaposition of "first" and "now" is further enhanced by the fact that they fall on the first heavy beat of a bar which lacks an anacrusis. That first note is also the tonal of the scale and is therefore very steady. It is accented because it is dotted and because the succeding note falls on a skip down to C (example 22).

These are the thematic contrasts round which the rest of the song is spun. In the second stanza (for B of the tune) it is implied that Meg's meakness and mildness belong to the past ("Wiser men than me's beguil'd"). The alliteration on *m* (*M*eg, *m*eek, *m*ild) has implications of both soft tenderness and suppressed anger, and Burns's correction in the Philadelphia manuscript (letter to Johnson, Nov. 1788) from "sweet" to "mild" shows that he was highly aware of the expressive effect of such an alliteration. It is used already in the first stanza (*M*aggy, *m*arried, *m*air) and is to be found also in the last, but there to express something negative, "*m*aggots' *m*eat". The B-section of the tune has a much more extrovert character with ascents, skips up and a higher register than in A. After the climax in B_3, which is the highest part of the tune, there is an effectful break before the theme of the refrain is resumed. Also, the poem stops short here: "Wiser men than me's beguil'd"—no more need be said, it is left to the listener's fantasy, only "Whistle o'er the lave o't". Johnson did not understand the effect of the lack of the upbeat, but added "*But* whistle" in line 4 and "*So* whistle" in line 8 to accommodate the last semi-quaver of the preceding bar (example 22). Thereby the short pause in which the implication lies is lost, and the refrain becomes too smooth and tame.[4]

The third stanza starts by implying happiness: "*How we* live, my Meg and me, / *How we* love and *how we* gree". Through the repetitions a sense of perfection is achieved, but, as in the preceding stanzas, through a little twist we are made to understand that the bliss is a rare guest ("I carena by how few may see"). The last stanza, finally, is the most outspoken. The music helps to build up the climax in line 3 (B_3) before the man stops and realizes that he cannot go any further:

> Wha I wish were maggots' meat,
> Dish'd up in her winding-sheet;
> I could write—but Meg maun see't—   *could*
> Whistle o'er the lave o't.—

[4] There is no MS-evidence that Burns should be responsible for these additional words. The

It is significant that these lines end on a tight-clipped *t*, which cuts off each line harshly and abruptly. Through this expressive plosive the man's suppressed frustration and anger is revealed. The first and third stanzas end on open syllables and the second fairly softly on a liquid plus a voiced plosive (*ld*). They are revealing only by subtle implication and have a sweet and polished *façade*, and it is only in the last stanza that the man shows his impatience more openly.

The theme of the man being fed up with his wife and his wish to see her dead is also to be found in "The weary Pund o' Tow" (360).[5] Here the wish is also fulfilled and more openly rejoiced in than in "Whistle o'er the lave o't". What is said by implication in the latter song is here reflected in a dramatic situation. If the thoughts and wishes are concealed in "Whistle o'er the lave o't", they are frankly outspoken in "The weary Pund o Tow". What the two songs have in common, apart from the marital theme, is the simplicity of the tune, the conversational character of the song and the concentration of the lyric expression within a short and tight-structured frame-work. "The weary Pund o' Tow" is more dramatic, however, and the attention is focused on action rather than on thinking. The tune is simple and its repetitive pattern and dotted rhythm is perceptively used for the conversational, expressive and dramatic diction of the poem. The internal rhymes, cutting the line in two halves, correspond to the repeated figure in the music. The rhyme on "tow" (*fibre of flax*) is used throughout the whole song and ties it together. "Tow" is also a significant word in the song as it is the reason for the argument between man and wife (the fact that she never finishes spinning it).

The chorus is important:

> The weary pund, the weary pund,
> The weary pund o' tow;
> I think my wife will end her life,
> Before she spin her tow.—

Its textual and melodic form endows the whole song with a sense of weariness with the kind of life and human relation that it depicts. Its tune has a very slow pace and with the heavy second beats it has a saraband-like rhythm which accents not only "weary" but also "pund". It is centred round the tonic, which gives it stability, and the tempo is slowed down by the internal rhymes cutting lines 1 and 3 in two phrases. The climax of the tune comes in bar 3, where it

fact that they are inserted only in stanzas 1 and 2 in *SMM*, which were printed *under* the notes, support my assumption that Johnson made the additions to accommodate "spare" notes.

[5] Kinsley points out that Burns's starting-point was the following stanza of a song in *The Charmer*, a collection of songs printed in 1782, which he was intimately acquainted with:

> I bought my woman and my wife half a pund of tow,
> I think 'twill serve them a' their life to spin as fast's as they dow;
> I thought it had been ended when scarce it was begun,
> And I believe my wife sall end her life and leave the two unspun ...

rises and gives an intenser colour to the third "weary pund" (see Ch. 2, example 2).

The lethargic heaviness of the expression of the chorus, the repetition of the phrase "the weary pund", the recurrence of the word "tow" also in the stanzas, and the evocative effect of the rhymes on the same word, all this turns the "weary pund o' tow" into a symbol of the dreariness of the married life in the song. What lies behind is the economic necessity of spinning the tow and the economic exploitation of the woman. The spinning of the tow is the extrinsic reason for the confrontation between man and wife, and it is also by that action that time is measured (lines 3—4).

The chorus is a comment on the present situation but also a foreshadowing of future events. As is hinted at in the chorus, the woman dies in the last stanza and the man rejoices: "At last her feet, I sang to see't, / Gaed foremost o'er the knowe" (*mound*). This stanza ends in the minor key (on the tone below the tonic), but the fact that the chorus is the conclusion of the song gives it an ironic twist, for it ends in the major. It thereby reinforces the joy felt by the man in stanza 4 and the song ends as the comedy it is. But the chorus is also important from a time aspect. Between stanzas 1 and 2 and between 3 and 4 there is a lapse of time, which the chorus serves to bridge. Especially between 3 and 4 this is important, for it is only against the passing of time that the happiness of the man seems really logical and is poetically justified. His "at last" is an outburst of relief after long waiting.

The central action and the climax of the song, the confrontation between the man and the woman, lies in stanzas 2 and 3. By making maximum poetical use of the expressive possibilities of the tune, Burns has caught the little domestic and comic drama in its essence. When the tune rises high and emphatically lands on the top note through a skip, there is also an explosion in the lyric, an explosion which is hardly as dramatic without the tune (example 23):

. . . .	
And ay she took the tither souk,	*the other suck*
To drouk the stourie tow.—	*soak; dusty*

. . . .	
She took the rock, and wi' a knock,	*distaff*
She brak it o'er my pow.—	*head*

"The weary Pund o' Tow" (360, SMM No. 350)   Example 23.

And   ay she took the tith-er souk, To drouk...
She   took the rock, and wi' a knock, She brak...

80

This explosion is prepared for in the first two lines of each stanza and although in the third stanza, these are dramatic, it is in the third line that something happens. With the "clipped" consonants (see Ch. 4, n. 10), the internal rhymes on *k* are particularly effective. The sound of the plosive and the subsequent abrupt stop, the high note, the pause inevitably ensuing before the last line, which is sung much lower—all this has a strong dramatic, pictorial and onomatopoeic effect. One can almost hear the sound of the wooden distaff being knocked against the man's head, see the unexpectedness of the woman's action, and feel the surprise of the man. His anger with her is conveyed through the conversational and interrupted phrasing of "Quoth I, for shame, [pause] ye dirty dame". She, of course, is furious at being bullied by her husband and tired of the slavery of domestic work, and the dammed up reaction was bound to come strongly and suddenly.

Another troublesome wife is the woman of "O ay my wife she dang me" (594). In the chorus she "dangs" (*beats*) her husband and she "bangs" her husband, and "dang" and "bang" are emphasized and prolonged as they fall on the minims of bars 2 and 4. "On peace and rest my mind was bent, / And fool I was I marry'd", says the man in the first stanza and there is a contrast between his former dreams and the present reality. The tune has a rising contour which gives a slight accent to "fool" and reaches its peak on "married", and the fact that he should have been foolish enough to marry is exactly what irritates the man. He differs from his husband-companions in the other marriage-songs, however, in being more passive and seeing no other way out but through his own death: "My pains o' hell on earth is past, / I'm sure o' bliss aboon, man" (*above*). Yet he does not seem to let his troubles on earth make him sorry, for his tune is cheerful with a major mode, lively tempo and a relaxed undotted rhythm.

"Song—Sic a wife as Willie's wife" (373) belongs to another genre and is, as Kinsley points out, "a fine example of the *grotesquerie* in which Scots poets have indulged since the time of Dunbar". It is the story about Willie Wastle and his wife, a woman who is "bow-hough'd" (*bandy-legged*), "hem-shin'd",[6] right-twisted, left-twisted, hump-breasted, hump-shouldered, one-eyed, five-teethed, bearded and clapper-tongued. It is a humorous song and a witty song. It does not deal with the relation between man and wife, nor has it got any kind of psychological insight. It says nothing about the man, but is a straight-forward description of the woman only. It does not depend on brevity and simplicity for its expression as do the songs discussed above, but instead it abounds in descriptive details, which build up a real caricature of the sturdy

---

[6] "hem-shin'd", i.e. "with shins shaped like *haims,* the curved pieces of wood or metal fixed over a draught-horse's collar" (Kinsley, p. 1576).

woman. It is therefore important that the tempo of the tune is slow and the rhythm uncomplicated, so that the text can carry through. There are several long words and double adjectives which would hardly have their striking effect in a quicker tempo and with a more complex tune. The lift in the second half should be noticed especially in the first stanza, as it distinguishes the introduction from the actual description of the woman. The lack of an upbeat is also important as it changes the accentuation of the poetic metre at some places. Line 11, for instance, would be formally scanned "Five rústy téeth, forbýe a stúmp" (*as well as*), whereas the musical rhythm reinforces the natural speech-rhythm: "Fíve rusty téeth, forbýe a stúmp". As that half-stanza already contains two more numbers ("She has an e'e, she has but *ane*, / Our cat has *twa*, the very colour"), both "ane" and "twa" being accented on the top-notes, the musical rhythm counterbalances this much more effectively than the poetic metre does by bringing out the figure "five". In stanza 3 more attention is given to the repeated "she" through the musical accentuation. This is a song to laugh at, to share the fun of, and to join in with, and in which the refrain gives the view-point of the detached observer: "Sic a wife as Willie's wife, / I wadna gie a button for her". We are not invited to be deeply engaged in it, but only to watch and enjoy its absurdities.

Less centred round the theme of marriage and dealing with an attitude to life rather than a specific situation or character is "I hae a wife o' my ain" (361).[7] Depending on brevity, simplicity and antitheses, this song advocates an uncomplicated way of living and a positive outlook on life. It displays the basic needs of life: love, money, freedom and happiness, and in four simple stanzas each of these aspects is presented. The first deals with love and marriage, conceived of in terms of faithfulness:

> I hae a wife o' my ain,
> I'll partake wi' naebody;
> I'll tak Cuckold frae nane,
> I'll gie Cuckold to naebody.—

Each line is a thought-contained unit, and in each stanza the first and third lines carry the basic statements, whereas the second and fourth are qualifications or explanations of these. The music reinforces this pattern, the first and third bars having ascending or high phrases, and the second and

---

[7] The song is probably modelled on the following old stanza cited by Kinsley:

> I hae a wife o' my awn,
> I'll be haddin' to naebody;
> I hae a pat and a pan,
> I'll borrow frae naebody.

fourth having arched and low phrases. These positive statements significantly come first and they end on long notes, carrying the monosyllabic rhymes, something which strengthens the impression of a self-confident, assured and optimistic outlook on life:

> I am naebody's lord,
>   I'll be slave to naebody;
> I hae a gude braid sword,
>   I'll tak dunts frae naebody.—   *blows*

The happy-go-lucky character of the song is also embodied in the syllabic setting, the simple and limited word-choice, and in the quick tempo of the tune. It has the same kind of light and energetic character as "Tam Glen" (see Ch. 3) and is set in the same time (9/8).[8] The preoccupation with the self (the repeated "I" and the lack of an upbeat emphasizing the pronoun) also points to a happy egotism which shuns no means to reach the personal freedom of body and mind. As Crawford aptly points out, the song expresses a *"petit bourgeois* attitude"[9] with its stress on a wife of one's own and on money.

Two songs view the marriage in perspective and reflect upon it, "The deuks dang o'er my daddie" (383) and "John Anderson my Jo" (302). The first is a dialogue between man and wife, where she complains about his growing sexual impotence ("An he is but a fusionless carlie, O" *dry old man*) and he retorts that she, too, has had her time ("I've seen the day, and sae hae ye"). The situation is dealt with in light and comical terms, and the major tune with its dotted, dancing rhythm (6/8) precludes any tragical dimensions. Although the aging couple has an argument about the "downa do" (*impotence*) that has come over the man, there are no undertones of frustration or ill-will.

Also reflecting on a life-long marriage, but expressing much deeper and more tender feelings, is "John Anderson my Jo" (302). In few songs does Burns reach such absolute perfection in the unity of music and poetry as in this. He took his start from the second stanza of an old song with a theme similar to that of "The deuks dang o'er my daddie" (the aging man's impotence), but changed it so that, in Kinsley's words, ". . . Sexual reminiscence is replaced by pride in a long faithfulness; Burns alters the tone from licentious complaint to affection, and over the same air he makes a new song for old age in which passion has turned to gentle companionship." The song is one of Burns's most famous and it has been more thoroughly analysed than any other song. Critics have commented upon the contrast between then and now and on

---

[8] Thorpe Davie draws attention to the three-times-three time of the song, but finds that it halts at alternate bars which makes it uncomfortable. Thorpe Davie, p. 172.

[9] Crawford, p. 283.

the correspondence of this with the lift in the second half of the tune. Kinsley puts it this way:

The air—something of a rant when it is played briskly—slows down into plaintive smoothness, with an even rhythm beautifully correspondent to quiet speech. The emphatic lift at the beginning of the fifth phrase expresses, almost as a sigh, the contrast in the poem between then and now; the controlled descent to the repeated final phrase expresses the assurance and calm of the song's ending.[10]

The embryo of this then-now antithesis is to be found in the second stanza of the old song set to the same tune in *MMC* (p. 142):

> John Anderson, my jo, John,
>   When first that ye began,
> Ye had as good a tail-tree,
>   As ony ither man;
> *But now* its waxen wan, John,
>   And wrinkles to and fro;
> [I've t]wa gae-ups for ae gae-down,
>   John Anderson, my jo.

By shortening the song from six to two stanzas Burns has concentrated the expression, the gist of which is emotional togetherness, and he has developed the unity between music and poetry as will be shown below.

In the first half-stanza the old woman is nostalgically thinking back, remembering how young and beautiful her husband used to be. The first musical phrase (A), in which the subject-matter in undramatically introduced, has an arched melodic contour, whereas the second (A¹) rises towards the end to prepare for the more intense second half-stanza. There the woman is taken from her dreams back to reality. The word "but", falling on a high upbeat, emphatically marks the transition from then to now:

A	John Anderson my jo, John,	
	When we were first acquent;	
A¹	Your locks were like the raven,	
	Your bony brow was brent;	*smooth*
B	*But now* your brow is beld, John,	
	Your locks are like the snaw;	
C	But blessings on your frosty pow,	*head*
	John Anderson my Jo.	

In his essay "The Music of the Heart" Kinsley notes that as "the second section of the air [i.e. Scottish airs in general] tends to lift—or, in Burns's phrase, take the 'high part'—the song-writer has his opportunities for contrast in the structure of a restricted musical form".[11] Burns has, as in so many other

[10] See also Crawford, p. 285; Thornton, *The Tuneful Flame*, p. 7.
[11] Kinsley, "The Music of the Heart", pp. 45—46.

84

songs, taken poetical advantage of this lift and made B in the lyric the highest emotional point. It marks the sudden awareness of past and present, of young and old, of colourful and colourless. The first half-stanza is a flash of recollection, emotionally painful when set against reality, but the course of life is accepted and therefore no bitterness is felt. Instead, on the terraced descent in phrase C of the tune, the woman expresses all her tender love and protection for her husband. There is only a touch of melancholy in it, due to the Aeolian mode (example 24). The woman's preoccupation in this stanza is with the name of her husband (cf. the old song cited above) and with the word "you" ("your" is mentioned five times in the stanza) which conveys a sense of deep concern for the other person.

"John Anderson my Jo" (302, SMM No. 260)   Example 24.

Your locks were like the raven, Your bony brow was brent;
But now your brow is beld, John, Your locks are like the snaw;
But blessings on your frosty pow, John Anderson my Jo.

Black and white and "brent" and "beld" are effectively juxtaposed in the form of inverted order and strikingly displayed against the shift in the music (notice also the alliterations):

> A[1]   Your *locks* were like the raven,
>   Your bony *brow* was brent;
> B   But now your *brow* is beld, John,
>   Your *locks* are like the snaw;

The music for "bony brow was brent" (bar 3 of A[1]) is exactly the same as for "now your brow is beld" (bar 1 of B) with the only difference that in B the melodic curve then rises higher than in A[1], thereby marking the reality of the "now" more intensely (example 24). This idea of repeating line 4 may be a reminiscence of the traditional song, where lines 4 and 5 are almost identical in the fourth and fifth stanzas. There, however, they serve as a link between the

85

two half-stanzas, carrying on the same theme, whereas Burns has used it for the effect of contrast.

The second stanza centers round "we" instead of "you", on the life together, and describes how the couple "clamb the hill" and spent "mony a canty day" (*pleasant*) together. But against this and on the lift in B the reality of the "now" is set:

Now we maun totter down, John,   *must*
And hand in hand we'll go;
And sleep the gither at the foot,   *together*
John Anderson my Jo.

The emphasis in the second half is no longer on "now" but on "we" (cf. "But *now*" in line 5 and "Now *we*" in line 13), as it falls on the first beat of the bar as well as on a dotted note. Also the significant word "down" in this line is emphasized through a dotted note. When the tune descends step by step in the last four-bar phrase, the poetry expresses peaceful resignation and in Crawford's words it "suggests finality, calm, the peace that passeth all understanding".[12] This finely perceptive song to John Anderson is the expression of constant and unflagging love, in spite of the changes of time, and of the tender love of somebody willing to accept ageing.

In the following chapter we shall turn to a group of songs in which sentiment again is the dominant feature. It ties up with Chapter 4 in that these sentiments are mostly expressed through the man, and in that the style is often influenced by that of eighteenth-century English poetry. Love still preponderates, but a new aspect is brought in and that is the aspect of nature. Love, or any kind of sentiment, is mingled with nature, and as we shall see the tunes may now not only enhance emotions but also suggest scenery.

---

[12] Crawford, p. 286.

Chapter 6

Nature and Sentiment

Burns wrote very few, if any, pure nature-songs. His interest in people and in the activities of life made descriptions of nature occupy a secondary position. Yet there are a large number of songs which have landscape-scenery, but in these songs nature is never there for its own sake. It is always mingled with sentiment, particularly love, and it serves as a foil to the feelings of the poet. Nature arouses his emotions, either because it is in sympathy with them, or because it is contrary to his state of mind. The changes in seasons, in weather and colours, the sound of the birds and the meandering rivers, the view of the hills and the mountains, all this may remind the poet of a past or a present love. It makes him reflect on his happiness or on his depression or think of the features of a beloved woman. Burns's concern in these songs is with the mingling of nature and emotions rather than with characterization or action. The music enhances the general sentiment of the lyric and is sometimes also evocative of the scenery. In some songs the description of nature dominates, in others it serves only as a framework to the description of a girl or the feelings of the poet.

In very few of these songs does Burns plunge straight into the central theme. Instead he leads us into it, and gently prepares for it by opening the song with a description of nature. In "Craigieburn-wood—A Song" (340) it is the awakening of the morning that sets forth a flow of emotions in the poet. These emotions are so overwhelming that the theme of nature is completely abandoned after two stanzas. The poet looks around, he sees the flowers and he hears the birds, but they only remind him of his unhappy love, the love which is to become the main theme of the song. The tune, "Craigieburn-wood", was one of Burns's favourites. It had never been printed before he "got it taken down from a country girl's singing" (Letter 557). He took much trouble over it and even sent a second and "a better set" of the tune to Johnson (Letter 503). With its rises and falls in major, its swing of the 6/8-time, its slow tempo and its emphatic upward leap of an octave in bars 3 and 7, it finely conveys the expression of sighing and yearning and wishful longing which is the predominant sentiment of the poem.

The form of the first part of the tune is AA, where the second A in stanzas 1—4 expresses grief and sorrow in contrast to the first, which is more positive.

This division into two contrasting sections is also marked by the word "but" in line 3 of each of those four stanzas. In the opening stanza the two themes of the beauties of nature and the depressed poet are effectively juxtaposed:

A   Sweet closes the evening on Craigieburn-wood,
      And blythely awaukens the morrow;
A   But the pride o' the spring in the Craigieburn-wood
      Can yield me nought but sorrow.—

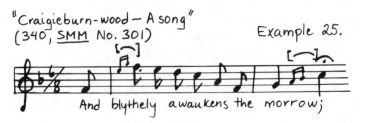

"Craigieburn-wood — A song"
(340, SMM No. 301)   Example 25.

And blythely awaukens the morrow;

There is an almost exuberant upward leap of an octave on the word "blythely" (bar 3, see example 25) in the first half, the same leap which expresses emotional pain on "yield" (bar 7) in the second (a dimension totally lost if the song is only read). In the second stanza, the song becomes more subjective: "I see the spreading leaves and flowers, / I hear the wild birds singing", the second line being more intense because of the leap. But the opposition to nature is still there. Nothing of what the poet sees or hears can mitigate his sorrow ("But pleasure they hae nane for me"). It only reinforces the sad memories of the past, and like an outcry of despair on the leap in bar 7, "care" painfully wrings his heart. In the third stanza the poet has become blind to nature and is now wholly engrossed in the thoughts of the girl: "I can na tell, I maun na tell, / I dare na for your anger". There is a crescendo of feeling from "I can" and "I maun", "can" and "maun" falling on the heavy, dotted first beats of the bars and "maun" lying higher than "can", to the climax in "I dare na for your anger", again effected by the leap to the top-note in bar 3. In the fifth stanza the amorous thoughts become agonizing:

To see thee in another's arms,
   In *love* to lie and languish:
'Twad be my dead, that will be seen,
   My heart wad brust wi' anguish!

"Love" is emphasized through the leap, but the effect is ironic, since that love is directed towards "another". The line is moulded on the soft and liquid *l* in "*love*", "*l*ie" and "*l*anguish" and is thereby contrasted to the much harsher sound in "hea*rt*" and "*br*ust", which mercilessly reminds the poet of the bitter

88

reality. It is interesting that Burns should use the expressive Scottish form "brust" instead of the comparatively weaker "burst" to accentuate the painful feeling. The sixth stanza, finally, sums up the wishes and dreams expressed by the poet throughout the song.

The air is a continuous reminder of the innermost feelings of the poet, but the longing and yearning is also defined in words in the chorus. This was taken from "an old foolish ballad" (*Notes,* p. 53) and was not originally connected with this tune. It has, however, been made an organic part of the song, expressing the nature of the "secret love". Intense in its high register and softly lulling in the 6/8-time, it is a gentle reminder of the ever-present wish of the poet. The emotional implications of this wish are varied through the rises and falls in the melodic curve, and it reaches its climax on the long, top-note (a dotted crotchet) in the fourth bar (taking "beyond"):

> Beyond thee, Dearie, beyond thee, Dearie,
> And Oh to be lying *beyond* thee!
> O sweetly, soundly, weel may he sleep,
> That's laid in the bed beyond thee.—

The song is a good illustration of the interaction between text and tune. The shape, mode and rhythm of the melody create the general sentiment of the song, but it is through the words that the musical expression becomes definite. The leap of an octave in bars 3 and 7 takes on a different character throughout the song: in stanza 1 it is sprightly with the word "blythely", in stanzas 2, 3 and 4 it serves an intensifying purpose (for "I hear", "I dare" and "I see"), and in stanzas 2 and 5 it becomes expressive of deeply felt grief (with "while care", "in love" and "my heart"). This shows how the same melodic figure may lend itself to different expressions depending on what words are joined to it.

In "The Banks o' Doon" (328 B) the themes of love and nature are more organically intertwined. Nature is present all the time to remind the woman of her grief. It becomes expressive and in the last half-stanza symbolic of it. The scene is set by a river, and the pentatonic air with its beautifully arched phrases evoke the sound of the slowly-flowing river accompanying the woman's sadness. As in "Craigieburn-wood" the tune has a rocking 6/8-time which gives it a sighing quality. But it also embodies anguish and despair. There is a subtle interplay of dotted and snapped quavers, which are very susceptible of pathos, and "pathos is certainly its native tongue" says Burns in a letter to Thomson (Letter 647). The rocking rhythm is slow and steady with heavy first and fourth beats (crotchets and dotted quavers, see example 26). In such a context the snaps become expressive of something uncomfortable, something which upsets the steady motion of the tune. They create an underlying feeling of disharmony and distress and this is particularly the case in the second half

(B), where the tune lifts and repeats the same "snapped" figure five times (example 27).

The first stanza introduces the bird and the blooming flowers in lines beautifully moulded on the consonants *b* and *f*. It also introduces the feelings of the woman, her resignation and her depression in the rhetorical questions:

A   Ye banks and braes o' bonie Doon,   *hill*
        How can ye bloom sae fresh and fair;
A¹   How can ye chant, ye little birds,
        And I sae weary, fu' o' care!

In this section (the form of the whole tune is AA¹BA¹) the air ascends from the tonic, returns, descends from it and returns again (example 26). There is a sense of security to which the second half provides a strong contrast:

B   Thou'll break my heart, thou warbling bird,
        That wantons thro' the flowering thorn:
A¹   Thou minds me o' departed joys,
        Departed, never to return.—

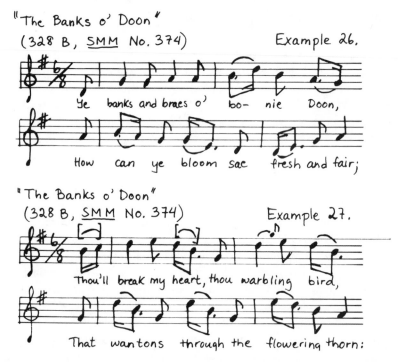

"The Banks o' Doon"
(328 B, SMM No. 374)   Example 26.

Ye banks and braes o' bo- nie Doon,

How can ye bloom sae fresh and fair;

"The Banks o' Doon"
(328 B, SMM No. 374)   Example 27.

Thou'll break my heart, thou warbling bird,

That wantons through the flowering thorn:

With the snaps and the repetitive melodic pattern this part of the tune is much more agitated. It centers round the fifth note of the scale in a persistent rising-falling figure, which reaches its climax in bar 4, where it starts one note higher (example 27). Also the lyric is much more active and dramatic here. The woman now turns to one bird, whose singing seems to pierce her heart, just as the melody is piercing on that repeated figure. When the tune resumes the opening theme (A¹), the lyric likewise returns to the resignation of the beginning, and in Crawford's words, "... When associated with the music, the repetition of 'departed' and the stock expression 'never to return' add immeasurably to the pathos."[1]

In the second stanza too, the dramatic impact comes in the second half, whereas the first is more passive. As in the first stanza it describes the scene with the singing bird and the blooming flower, but this time it is more specific. The image of the rose is introduced, and the bird now explicitly sings "o' its Luve", which reminds the woman: "And fondly sae did I o' mine". With the agitation in the second half of the tune she bitterly recalls the deception of the "fause Luver":

B	Wi' lightsome heart I pu'd a rose,	
	Fu' sweet upon its thorny tree;	
A¹	And my fause Luver staw my rose,	*stole*
	But, ah! he left the thorn wi' me.—	

Although her heart is "lightsome", the unsettled quality of the air and the collocation of the words "sweet" and "thorny" foreshadow the disaster in the last two lines. The song ends in resignation, a resignation which is effectively reinforced by the music through the return to the A-theme.

There are two earlier versions of the song, both written to the tune "Cambdelmore". The second of these (328 A), which differs from the first only in the first stanza, was meant to go into *SMM*, but was eventually revised (328 B, analysed above) to suit the tune "Caledonian Hunt's Delight" instead. The second version (328 A), which is written for a tune consisting of three parts taking "three Stanzas of four lines each, to go through the whole tune" (Letter 441), was for a long time held by the critics to be the better from a poetical point of view because of its more concise and restrained diction. Later critics have, however, drawn attention to the tunes and shown that the revision (328 B), regarded as a song, is far superior to the second version. Thorpe Davie says that it is "regrettable that the tune of the first version [i.e. 328 A for "Cambdelmore"] is so feeble, with its tendency to sit down for a rest at each alternate bar, but it is an inescapable fact, which puts out of court any claim to superiority over the second version [i.e. 328 B for "Caledonian Hunt's Delight"]".[2] To this comment on the pedestrian four-beat rhythm of "Cambdelmore" may be added that the rhythm of "Caledonian Hunt's

[1] Crawford, p. 291.
[2] Thorpe Davie, p. 169.

Delight" is better suited to the iambs of the lyric. In his revision Burns has also dispensed with the superfluous third and sixth stanzas "which are only rhetorical amplifications to suit the three parts of *Cambdelmore*", as Kinsley notes, and thereby he arrived at a more poignant and dramatic contrast between the two halves of each stanza. Finally I quote Crawford who sums up the merits of the revision thus:

As a matter of fact, when it is sung to the melody for ever associated with it, the extra syllables cease to be redundant, and the song emerges as quite different in mood from the other two. When considered as a *song,* and not merely as a verbal pattern, it becomes a beautifully poignant expression of love's melancholy, and the contrast between the bird's glee and the lover's pain emerges far more clearly than in either of the other versions.[3]

Also set by a river is "The banks of the Devon" (183), a song "composed on a charming girl, a Miss Charlotte Hamilton" (*Notes,* p. 29). This girl is compared to a flower and the expression of the song is no longer grief, but tender and protective devotion. The tune is Gaelic and Burns writes that he "first heard the air from a lady in Inverness, and got the notes taken down for this work [SMM]" (*Notes,* p. 29). Again the musical time is 6/8, and with its slow, rocking lilt and its rhythmical pattern, which is kept unvaried throughout the song, the air creates an atmosphere of peace and gentleness. The phrases are long and the melody in the first half meanders in two big arches. The lyric here describes the beautiful scenery along the banks of the river (notice words like "pleasant", "clear-winding", "green-spreading" etc.) and singles out one of the flowers as being the "bonniest". In the second half there is a beautiful and subtle change at the lift of an octave. In this high, more intense register the poet says his little prayer to the flower:

> Mild be the sun on this sweet-blushing Flower,
> In the gay, rosy morn as it bathes in the dew;
> And gentle the fall of the soft, vernal shower,
> That steals on the evening each leaf to renew!

Because of the lack of an upbeat there is an expressive emphasis on the word "mild", so important in the context, and the repeated lifts in bars 9, 11 and 13 bring out the words "sun", "morn" and "fall", which all carry pleasant associations. The first half of the stanza is purely descriptive and reflective, whereas this is an active, but gentle wish for all the good to come to the "sweet-blushing Flower": "Mild be the sun" and "gentle the fall".

In the second stanza the poet addresses the destructive forces in nature and bids them stay away from the delicate flower. The high part of the tune is now proud and boasting with the words "exult" and "triumphant" falling on the

[3] Crawford, pp. 290—91.

92

top-notes: "Let Bourbon *exult* in his gay, gilded Lillies, / And England *triumphant* display her proud Rose". When, in the last four-bar phrase, the air resumes the melodic material of the first half, the lyric returns to the description of the simple little flower as a contrast to the artificiality expressed in the lines just quoted. The poetic diction of the song is somewhat affected and in the second stanza rather pompous. It is heavily clogged with words, and adjectives especially seem to be crammed in to fill out the dactylic lines. Notice for instance the double-adjectives in lines 1, 2, and 5 and phrases like "gay, rosy morn", "soft, vernal shower", "chill, hoary wing" and "gay, gilded Lillies". "Craigieburn-wood" and "The Banks o' Doon" are therefore more successful as songs because of their more direct and simple language.

Burns pays his romantic compliment also to the river Afton in the song "Afton Water" (257). In a letter to Mrs. Dunlop there is a note about it:

There is a small river, Afton, that falls into Nith, near New Cumnock; which has some charming, wild, romantic scenery on its banks.—I have a particular pleasure in those little pieces of poetry such as our Scots songs &c. where the names and landskip-features of rivers, lakes, or woodlands, that one knows, are introduced.—I attempted a compliment of that kind, to Afton as follows: I mean it for Johnson's Musical Museum.—(Letter 310)

The song is in praise of the river and a lullaby to Burns's Highland Mary, who, according to the legend, died a tragic death after a short but romantic affair with Burns. When read without its tune the poem seems a rather dull and pedestrian affair. It is very long, the poetic language is conventional and the stiff regularity of the metre is boring. However, in the tune lies the sentiment which Burns has not succeeded in conveying through words only. There is a lilting and rocking in the triple rhythm (3/4), the undotted notes and the alternation between crotchets and quavers, which finely fits the theme of the slowly-flowing river and which transforms the lyric into a tender lullaby for the sleeping Mary. The shape of the melody is also important for the impact of the song. It is undulating and there are no abrupt changes of register, no skips and leaps, the lift in B being very undramatic. The intervals are narrow, and the melody moves mostly by seconds and thirds. There is also an upbeat which makes the onset more gentle. The form of the tune is AA^{1}BA^1, where the recapitulation of A^1 has the effect of a coming to rest after the gentle, but intense, ascent in B.

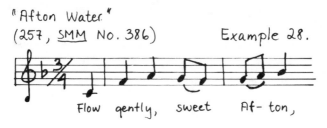

"Afton Water"
(257, SMM No. 386)   Example 28.

Flow gently, sweet Af-ton,

In the first stanza the motif is established which will be taken up again in the last stanza:

A	*Flow gently,* sweet Afton, among thy green braes,	*hills*
A[1]	*Flow gently,* I'll sing thee a song in thy praise;	
B	My Mary's asleep by thy murmuring stream,	
A[1]	*Flow gently,* sweet Afton, disturb not her dream.	

The recurring phrase in the lyric is no doubt suggested by a repeated figure in the music (example 28). In the above-mentioned letter to Mrs. Dunlop, where an early version of the song is to be found, the second line has "And grateful" instead of "Flow gently". The fact that Burns changed this line shows that he was highly aware of the musical pattern and wanted the verbal one to correspond to it. Through this device the poetical phrase is strongly imprinted on the listener and the melodic tag becomes associated with the gently-flowing river Afton. The return to A[1] after the lift in B is particularly expressive in this stanza as it forms a kind of frame of protectiveness round the theme of the sleeping Mary: "Flow gently, sweet Afton, disturb not her dream". Although a somewhat lengthy creation, the song is a good example of what Bronson calls parallel expressions of one emotion (see above, p. 29), which he regards as being the best type of textual setting of a tune. Each stanza is a variation of the same theme, the gently-flowing river and the beautiful countryside around mingled with the thoughts of Mary, "asleep by thy murmuring stream".

"A Song" (274), too, is devoted to the memory of Highland Mary. Here the "lingering Star" first reminds the poet of his former love, but his memories soon take him to "the winding Ayr" and its surroundings. The tune is beautiful, although somewhat unimaginative with its lack of variation, but the lyric is overelaborated and the song therefore lacks a concentrated impact. This Burns seems to have been aware of himself, for in a letter to Mrs. Dunlop he complains that he is "too much interested in the subject of it [the poem], to be a Critic in the composition" (Letter 371), and later he would suggest another tune for it ("Hughie Graham", Letter 557). Daiches points out that the poem is written in English and that its style is rhetorical and therefore not very characteristic of Burns. He finds that "it is a skilful but strained production, and the emotion is wrought up to a pitch that verges on hysteria".[4] Technically it is a bad fit, too. Many unstressed words, like prepositions, articles and feminine endings fall on accented notes, e.g. "with" in line 1, "the" in line 2, "ush*erest*" in line 3, and "my" in line 4.

A river may not only remind the poet of a past love or of a dear lassie, it can also evoke nostalgic feelings for the native country and for friends, as it does in "The Banks of Nith" (229). This song is written with the idea of "a young

---

[4] Daiches, *Robert Burns,* p. 302.

Gentleman perhaps going abroad" (Letter 265), and the two contrasting sections of the tune effectively juxtapose the conflicting emotions in the man: love for his country and despair at having to leave it. The first half-stanza is descriptive and is about the proudly-flowing Thames and, on the repetition of the musical phrase, about its opposite, the sweetly-flowing Nith. This part of the tune (AA) embodies a sense of the continuous motion of the river, as well as that of something constant and unchanging. Its tempo is slow and the tune leans heavily on the first and third beats, which are also the long notes of the bar. The tune is pentatonic and with an undulating melodic contour, it balances around the tonic in the plagal range. Constancy is also epitomized in the stately-standing "royal cities" and in the link with the past in the line "Where Cummins ance had high command". The second half-stanza is personal and reveals the despair of the young man:

> When shall I see that honor'd Land,
> That winding Stream I love so dear!
> Must wayward Fortune's adverse hand
> For ever, ever keep me here.

With that outburst the tune (BB) assertively ascends and it now lies within the authentic range. It rises to "see", it falls, and it leaps up to "Land" before it descends to the theme of the first section and the thought of the "winding Stream". For the second rhetorical question the melody rises anew before it drops resignedly on the falling melody with the repeated "ever".

The second stanza displays the same kind of contrast between the two halves. In the first there is a contemplation of the beautiful Nith and its surroundings ("How lovely, Nith, thy fruitful vales") and in the second there are the gloomy thoughts at having to leave it all: "Tho' wandering, now, must be my doom, / Far from thy bonie banks and braes". The accents on "now" and "doom", effected by the peaks in the melodic shape, emphasize the opposition between past joy and present despondency. Reinforced by the energy of the rising tune there comes, finally, the last wish: "May there my latest hours consume, / Amang the friends of early days!"

A less homogeneous example of Burns's predilection for mingling landscape with sentiment is found in the early "Song" (4), written in *1CPB* in April 1784. The air of this song is slow with a soft alternation between undotted crotchets and quavers. It is major, it has an undulating shape and a second half which lies high and has more descisively rising phrases. But it is only in the first two stanzas that Burns takes poetic advantage of the potentialities of the tune. The first stanza, for the low section, is soft. With its *l*'s and *m*'s, its dark vowels, its setting by a river, and its undramatic word-choice, it finely blends with the undulations of the tune:

> Behind yon hi*ll*s where *L*ugar *fl*ows,
> '*M*ang *m*oors an' *m*osses *m*any, O,
> The wintry sun the day has clos'd,
> And I'll awa to Nanie, O.

The name "Lugar" of the river was preferred by Burns to "Stinchar" and "Girvan" (his first choices) for its being "the most agreable modulation of syllables" (Letter 511), which shows with what awareness he listened to the sound not only of the music but also of the words. With the rises in the second half of the tune he lets the wind suddenly blow "loud an' shill" and the night turn "mirk and rainy" (*dark*), and against this bleak scene the lover's protestation is effectfully set: "But I'll get my plaid an' out I'll steal, / An' owre the hill to Nanie, O". After that the theme of nature is discarded for a rather conventional description of Nanie (stanzas 3 and 4) and a presentation of the laddie (stanzas 5 and 6). The poetry seems less successfully adapted to the expression of the tune here, as it does not change its theme and sentiment to match the rises and intensification of the second half. It is only in the conclusion of the song (stanzas 7 and 8) that Burns again makes use of the lift in the tune: the last stanza expresses a care-free abandon, a joy, and a love-assertion, which goes very well with the extrovert character of the tune:

> Come weel come woe, I care na by,   *don't care about it*
> I'll tak what Heav'n will sen' me, O;
> Nae ither care in life have I,
> But live, an' love my Nanie, O.

The lack of thematic homogeneity is even more apparent in "Yon wild mossy mountains" (163). The first three stanzas of this song describe the natural scenery round the "wild, mossy mountains" and how the poet loves being there, "For there, by a lanely, sequestered stream, / Resides a sweet Lassie, my thought and my dream". These stanzas suit the general mood of the tune with its modal feel and the little semi-quaver figure in bar 13, reminiscent of a piper's tune. The last three stanzas, on the other hand, present the lassie in a conventional, idealizing, and artificial way and are only very loosely connected with the first three stanzas. The repetition of the third and fourth lines of each stanza, necessary to cover the length of the tune, is tedious and the setting is clumsy with weak syllables and words on accented beats (e.g. "mos*sy*" in line 1, "*the* youth" in line 2, "foam*ing*" in line 10). The song has no unity and it lacks the simplicity so essential for a song.

Another, very early song which describes nature and then unexpectedly introduces a girl in it is "Song, composed in August" (2), written for a tune called "I had a horse, I had nae mair". With its utilitarian outlook on nature and its overloaded and mannered diction (Kinsley shows that Burns was strongly influenced by Pope and Thomson here), this poem does not blend in with the simplicity of the tune. Burns has not taken full poetical advantage of its expression and he has fitted the words rather clumsily to the melody. It is, for example, bad setting to put conjunctions and prepositions on emphatic lifts as in the first bar ("Now westlin winds, *and* slaught'ring guns", "The Pairtrick lo'es *the* fruitfu' fells"). The last two stanzas, however, match the expression of the tune much better. Here the stiff description of the landscape is discarded and the poet tells of his feelings of love for the girl Peggy. The diction is simpler and the slow major tune with its expressive upward leaps and assertive ascent at the end intensifies these feelings, and there is a stronger unity between text and tune.

"Bessy and her spinning wheel" (365) expresses the content of a girl sitting at her spinning-wheel, and in the first stanza it does so in a fairly simple and unpretentious way ("O leeze me on my spinnin-wheel, / And leeze me on my rock and reel"). But in the second stanza the song slips into an artificial neo-classical style, describing the surrounding nature in a sort of rococo-manner. The tune, which finely sustains the first stanza with its lift in the second half giving added expression to "I'll set me down and sing and spin", now seems estranged from the poetic diction and theme. In the first stanza the poem expresses the sentiment of the girl, something which can correspond with the musical expression, but in the rest of the song the artificial description of the landscape dominates and the tune seems little more than an accompaniment to the poem.

In "I love my Jean" (227), written to Burns's wife, Jean Armour, the poet describes how he likes the west, "For there the bony Lassie lives, / The Lassie I lo'e best" and how he sees his Jean "in the dewy flowers" and hears her "in the tunefu' birds". The tune is long (it covers the whole poem) and has a somewhat jerky melodic contour which makes it difficult to sing. It builds up to a nice climax, however, in the last stanza, where the poet's repeated "I see her" and "I hear her", falling on the lowest section of the tune, lead up to the exuberance of the last four lines:

> There's not a bony flower, that springs
> By fountain, shaw, or green;   *small wood*
> There's not a bony bird that sings
> But minds me o' my Jean.—

Here the tune lifts high, enhancing the joy felt by the loving poet, but then drops to end the song on a more intimate note.

In "She says she lo'es me best of a' " (457) the beautiful girl is described in the first two stanzas, and in the third she is set in natural surroundings ("There, dearest Chloris, wilt thou rove / By whimpling burn and leafy shaw" *meander-*

ing stream). Also this song is a rather stylized creation and Burns himself would later complain about it and say that to have a Greek name in a Scottish song would be "a high incongruity" (Letter 689). Yet the unusual tune gives the song a certain refreshing swing, or as Thorpe Davie puts it, the "sheer momentum [of the tune] conceals the fact that the verbal imagery is sometimes commonplace".[5] The text of "The Rosebud" (213), although rather commonplace, has tenderness and simplicity and a sense of structure, which, however, is lost when it is sung to the rather characterless and ungainly tune. The first pair of stanzas describes the rosebud, the second the linnet and the third is a comparison of the young Jeany, for whom the song was written, with the bird and the flower. But the fact that each stanza has to be repeated twice to cover the tune has a cumbrous effect on the poem and the fusion of lyric and tune does not seem organic in this song. Equally at odds with the character of the tune is "Where braving angry Winter's storms" (182), which is also very difficult to sing for the average singer as it covers two whole octaves. Being only a string of clichés, a genuine feeling behind the words is lacking. Finally, the beloved may also be compared to nature, as in "The Posie" (372), which is a conventional enumeration of flowers connected with the woman and symbolizing her assets and set to a simple and light-tripping tune.

As has been shown in "The Banks of Nith", the emotions reflected in nature are not always those of love for a woman. In "My heart's in the Highlands" (301) the protagonist sings about his love for his country: "My heart's in the Highlands, my heart is not here; / My heart's in the Highlands a chasing the deer" (in the interleaved *SMM* Burns states that the "first half-stanza of this song is old; the rest is mine", see *Notes,* p. 48). The song is a farewell-song with the word "farewell" emphatically repeated four times in stanza 3, but it is a farewell without sadness. The words imply a feeling of both joy and pride and the beautiful major tune with its optimistically rising phrases reinforces this expression.

In "Song" (122) the feelings are the reverse. Here the "gloomy night" and the "wild, inconstant blast" poignantly remind the poet that he has to leave his home-country and "the bonie banks of *Ayr*" (Burns's italics). It is a highly biographical song, written when Burns had decided to emigrate to Jamaica. He had taken farewell of his friends, and this song was the last he thought he would ever write in Caledonia (Letter 125). The song is one of the most melancholy in Burns's whole production. The minor tune (Aeolian) expresses painful grief in large skips and sudden transitions to the high register, and it conveys a sense of resignation and despondency through falling phrases and undotted rhythm. The poem indulges in bleak adjectives, desolate nouns and

[5] Thorpe Davie, p. 173.

98

despairing verbs to reinforce the sense of affliction, and the shape of the melody expressively and dramatically brings out some of these words in a way that a mere reading of the poem would not do. The form of the tune is ABCB, where C is the high section:

A   The gloomy night is gath'ring fast,
      Loud roars the *wild*, inconstant blast,
B   You murky cloud is foul with *rain*,
      I see it driving o'er the plain;
C   The Hunter now has left the moor,
      The scatt'red coveys meet secure,
B   While here I wander, prest with *care*,
      Along the lonely banks of *Ayr*.

Burns has used the sudden return to the low register, from C to B, very effectively in this stanza. The first three couplets are descriptive, with a due intensification in the third because of the lift in the tune. The poet looks around, he sees and feels surrounding nature, which is so much in sympathy with his mood. Then, as a striking contrast to the description of the scattered coveys securely gathering, the poet is reminded that he has to leave his country and his mood drops with the fall in the tune.

In the following stanzas the high, more intense section of the tune (C) is effectively used to carry the poet's personal feelings. In the second stanza the first half is descriptive and the second personal. The strong reaction of the poet to nature around him is imprinted on the listener through the dramatic lift in C: "Chill runs my blood to hear it rave, / I think upon the stormy wave". In the third stanza the contrast is that between something descriptive and something personal. The second half-stanza is here clearly marked off from the first by the word "but". In the last stanza the first half is a farewell to nature and the second a farewell to friends. The refrain of the song is the recurring and haunting thought in the poet's mind. Throughout the song it intensifies from "Along the lonely banks of *Ayr*" over "Far from the bonie banks of *Ayr*" to "To leave the bonie banks of *Ayr*", finally to reach the climax in the last stanza (the italicizing of "Ayr" in these lines is Burns's):

      Farewell, my friends! farewell, my foes!
      My peace with these, my love with those—
      The bursting tears my heart declare,
      Farewell, the bonie banks of *Ayr*!

The poetry in itself is hardly original with its conventional and sometimes melodramatic diction, but the song is a very good example of how Burns could interpret musical expression and adjust the poetic organization to the structure of the tune.

Similar in poetic sentiment but having a much lighter expression because of the tune is "The lazy mist" (234). It is a song which also describes a rather bleak scene, reflecting the state of mind of the poet. It is winter, the "forests are leafless", the colours are pale and brown, and there is a "lazy mist", "Concealing the course of the dark winding rill". Seeing that "all the gay foppery of Summer is flown" the poet is reminded of the flight of time and the flight of fate and, on the return to the low register of the tune, he turns to himself: "Apart let me wander, apart let me muse, / How quick Time is flying, how keen Fate pursues". The form is AABA[1] and the contrast between B and A[1] reinforces the opposition, but also the parallel, between the decaying state of nature and the depressed mind of the poet, something which the verbal pattern in itself cannot convey so poignantly. A reader will read on in the same unvaried metre, whereas the music forces him to a short pause, and, most important, to a change of emotional register.

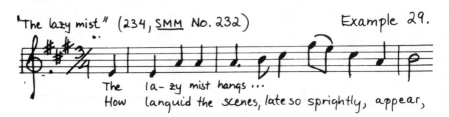

"The lazy mist" (234, SMM No. 232)   Example 29.

The   la-zy mist hangs ...
How   languid the scenes, late so sprightly, appear,

The major tune has a light triple rhythm and therefore also less tension than "Song" (122), which is minor and has a four-beat rhythm. It enlivens the gloom of the lyric and it also has some finely expressive pictorial effects. Notice for example how nicely the word "hangs" really "hangs", because it falls on a dotted crotchet, which is also the first beat of the bar (example 29). Through this device a sense of heaviness is conveyed, like that of the mist itself. In line 3 "sprightly" gets a push because it falls on an upward leap (example 29). The word becomes "sprightly" because of the energy needed for that leap and for the singer's enunciation of the cluster of the three initial consonants. In line 6 the word "foppery" naturally and lightly glides in on the quavers, whereas when read, it only seems to disturb the metre.

The second stanza, which continues the thought in lines 7—8 ("Apart let me wander" etc.), is less successful. It is abstract, pompous and rhetorical, and therefore does not fuse so easily with the expression of the music. Burns called this song (234) and "A Mother's Lament for the loss of her only Son" (233) "two melancholy things, which I tremble lest they should too well suit the tone of your present feelings" (Letter to Dr. Blacklock, 287). "A Mother's Lament" is one of Burns's least successful pieces. Loaded with conventional phraseology and set to a very complex tune, it has little merit.

100

Melancholy also are "Raving winds around her blowing" (207) and "Musing on the roaring Ocean" (208), both written for Gaelic tunes, and both very stylized and stodgy. The former is very monotonous with its repeated musical phrases, its slow tempo, its rhymed couplets, accented on the falling cadences at each two-bar phrase, and its antithetical pattern ("Farewell"—"Hail", "Sunshine days"—"gloomy night", "Past"—"Future"). The latter has a beautiful tune, but the lyric fails to respond to it, and as Kinsley points out "the mere repetition of the air hardly gives an adequate set to his [Burns's] eight-line stanza".

Most of the songs discussed so far have been either songs of tender feelings or songs of moody thoughts. There has been a sense of introversion about many of them, and reflectingly, never light-heartedly, emotions have mingled with aspects of nature. The language in these songs has often been very pretentious and artificial, the poems being closer to the English neo-classical style than to the Scottish folk-idiom. There is, however, a group of nature-songs which has a more extrovert character. They are love-songs, and in all of them joy is the dominant quality. The season is always spring or summer, and nature either sings with the happy lover, or the lassie is compared with it. The language is less mannered, the songs often take their start from a traditional line or two, and a chorus may serve to keep up the light tone and give the song the character of a folk-song.

Abounding with joy is the gracious little song "Bonie Bell" (379). It rejoices in spring and it rejoices in love. It is spun round the cyclic change of the seasons and there is a sense of continuous motion in the song. The tune, in triple time, is light and dancing. It is built up on major thirds and it rises positively at the beginning of each new phrase. The words are simple with verbs expressing activity ("comes", "flies", "breaks forth" etc.) and an abundance of adjectives giving pleasant association ("smiling", "rejoicing", "bonny"). The whole of the first stanza is devoted to the season of spring, where lines 1—4 describe the coming in of spring and lines 5—6 capture the cycle of one day in a nutshell: "Fresh o'er the mountains breaks forth the morning, / The ev'ning gilds the Ocean's swell". The rising musical phrase, giving "forth" an extra push, expressively illustrates the lively activity in nature. In the last two lines, finally, the poet's love for his Bonie Bell is compared to the happy reawakening of nature: "All Creatures joy in the sun's returning, / And I rejoice in my Bonie Bell". In the second stanza, with a wonderful sense of structure, the first four lines describe all four seasons, starting from summer and coming back to spring, and the last four form the synthesis and the gist of the song: the contrast between the cyclic change of nature and the constancy of the poet's love (notice how the internal rhymes enhance the sense of lightness):

> Thus seasons dancing, life advancing,
>> Old Time and Nature their changes tell,
> But never ranging, still unchanging,
>> I adore my Bonie Bell.

"Lovely Polly Stewart" (579) is another light-tripping love-song, commonplace in its lyric expression, yet attractive thanks to its lively and cheerful tune. The beloved is conventionally compared to a flower, but:

> The flower it blaws, it fades, it fa's,
>> And art can ne'er renew it;
> But Worth and Truth eternal youth
>> Will gie to Polly Stewart.—

With its chorus the song has a light-hearted character, and it passes like the flower, without leaving any deeper impressions on the listener.

"I'll ay ca' in by yon town" (574, *house, farm*) is the song of the contented lover on his way to his lass. His heart brims over and in a very infatuated way he rejoices in the secrecy of the love ("There's nane sall ken, there's nane sall guess, / What brings me back the gate again" *know*). The shortness of the song (two stanzas and a chorus), the light-tripping, major reel-tune, the exuberance of the melodic skips in the chorus, and the finished simplicity of the poetic diction make this a very impressionistic expression of happy love. Its structure implies also a physical expression of joy and impatient love and Crawford suggests that this is one of the songs which Burns said he composed on horseback. In Crawford's words "rhythm, words and melody combine to render a lover's mood as he gallops joyously towards his sweetheart's farm".[6] The song by far surpasses Burns's second version of the same theme, "Song" (488) which is a more artificial and pretentious creation. The latter has the blend of nature and love—the flowers and birds are blest because they are near the beloved, the sun shines and it is spring—but it seems an unnecessarily long exercise in variations of a theme.

In "The birks of Aberfeldey.—Composed on the spot" (170) each stanza gives a new aspect of the beauty of summer; it "blinks on flowery braes" (*hills*) and plays "o'er the chrystal streamlets", the birds sing "blythely", the "braes ascend like lofty wa's" and the "hoary cliffs are crown'd wi' flowers". Surrounded by this the poet feels "blest wi' love" and with his lassie. The chorus is old (Kinsley points out that Burns took it from an old lover's dialogue), and it reinforces the sense of joy and reminds one of the lassie: "Bony lassie will ye go, will ye go, will ye go; / Bony lassie will ye go to the birks of Aberfeldey." The tune is major, lively, and has assertively ascending phrases conveying a sense of happiness. Yet the song does not have the con-

---

[6] Crawford, p. 266.

centration and structure of "Bonie Bell" or "I'll ay ca' in by yon town" and it is, as Kinsley rightly remarks, too crammed with words for the swiftly running melody. William Montgomerie is of the opinion that Burns has in fact spoiled the old song, which has a simpler verbal pattern with less thematical material, repetitions being used a lot. With Burns's introduction of an abundance of ideas and especially of adjectives (and then several double-adjectives) he finds that it loses all its virtue.[7]

A simpler song is the "Song.—Composed at Auchtertyre on Miss Euphemia Murray of Lentrose" (179) which is well balanced and kept within stricter bounds. It does not dance like "Bonie Bell" or "The birks of Aberfeldey" because of a more controlled rhythm, and the chorus, in spite of its repetitions of the word "blythe", strikes a less care-free note. In the stanzas the girl is compared with different aspects of nature, with the trees and the flowers, with the birds and the lambs. This part of the tune has a cheerful quality which suits the description of the bonny lassie very well. It is major, it lies in the high register, and it has upward leaps and arched melodic phrases. Compared with the chorus (see below) it also has a greater variety of thematic material. These stanzas are all patterned in close correspondence with the musical phrases.

'Song.— Composed at Auchtertyre '
(179, SMM No. 180)   Example 30

The Highland hills I've wander'd wide, And o'er the lawlands I hae been;

With the exception of the third, each stanza starts with two similarly structured lines. Each line is a thought-contained unit and in stanzas 2 and 4 they are also main clauses. This corresponds to the phrase-pattern of the tune, which has the character also of two two-bar phrases, rather than of one four-bar phrase. The last two lines, on the other hand, form one long clause where the second line is subordinate to the first and the corresponding last phrase of the tune is now one four-bar phrase. In stanzas 1 and 4 the turning-point is moreover marked by the word "but". Just as the music takes a new start by a repeated upward leap (example 30), the lyric also repeats itself before it comes to the summing up in the last two lines:

> *The Highland hills* I've wander'd wide,
> *And o'er the lawlands* I hae been;
> *But* Phemie was the blythest lass
> That ever trode the dewy green.

(Stanza 4)

[7] Montgomerie, pp. 26—27.

The chorus is stricter with the reiteration of the fifth note of the scale and it is less extrovert because of the falling phrases, the limited melodic material, and the minor quality. Burns took his start from the chorus in an old drinking-song to the tune of "Andrew an' his cutty gun":

> Blyth, blyth, blyth was she,
>> Blyth was she butt and ben;   back and front
> And well she loo'd a Hawick gill,   glass of whisky
> And leugh to see a tappit hen.   laughed; bottle
>> (Quoted by Kinsley)

This he changed into a chorus which is more tightly and consciously knit to the structure and phrasing of the tune than the old one:

> Blythe, blythe and merry was she,
>> Blythe was she but and ben: in the outer and inner room
> Blythe by the banks of Ern,
>> And blythe in Glenturit glen.—

The most important note of this part of the tune is the B. It recurs four times, it has the longest note-value, it falls on the first beat of the bar and that beat has no anacrusis, and finally, it stands out because of the large interval down to the next note. In Burns's chorus the word "blythe" falls four times on this weighty note (see Ch. 2, example 3) but only twice in the old one. This is the adjective which Burns wants to imprint on the listener, for this is the major quality of the girl he describes. As it comes in the chorus, and then with such emphasis, the listener is continuously reminded of it. The rhythmical balance also is more marked in Burns's version than in the old one. The latter has "Blyth, blyth, blyth was she", whereas Burns writes "Blythe, blythe and merry was she". "And merry" counterbalances the repeated "blythe" better than the mere third repetition of the word does. It also matches the music better. "Merry" effectively falls on a snap in the SMM setting, a rhythm which suits its speech-rhythm perfectly.

Of a gentler kind is "The Gardener wi' his paidle—or, The Gardener's march" (291), a nature- and love-song which is spun round the old title of the air (Notes, p. 45). Two beautifully arched four-bar phrases (AA¹, the form of the whole tune is AA¹BA¹) correspond to the poetical organization: the onset of a new musical phrase takes a new sentence in the lyric (stanzas 1 and 3):

> A When rosy May comes in wi' flowers
>> To deck her gay, green, spreading bowers;
> A¹ Then busy, busy are his hours,
>> The Gardener wi' his paidle.—   paddle

The tune is major, it has a slow, undotted rhythm varying between crotchets and quavers, and there are no abrupt leaps or changes of register. "The chrystal waters gently fa' " on a terraced descent (in B) bringing out the word "chrystal" and its crisp cluster of consonants on the top-note. The birds are all merry and there are colours and scents to be seen and felt. The song describes the coming in of the month of May (stanzas 1 and 2) but also the coming in of a spring-day (stanza 3), and when the air has those falling figures in its second half (B), the day draws to its close (stanza 4) and the sun sets: "When Day, ex-piring in the west, / The curtain draws of Nature's rest". Then the melody goes up again, it expresses more activity and suitably ends with the lover flying to the arms of his lassie.

There remain two songs to be considered, two songs which do not connect nature with any particular sentiment. The first is "Up in the Morning Early" (200) and the second "Cauld is the e'enin blast" (601), both songs dealing with winter, although the second with an unexpected humorous twist at the end. In "Up in the Morning Early" the chorus is old (*Notes*, p. 28), but changed a little by Burns to fit the air. Around this chorus he has spun a lyric about the blow-ing wind, the winter birds and the long winter nights:

> Cauld blaws the wind frae east to west,
>   The drift is driving sairly;   *snow; violently*
> Sae loud and shill's I hear the blast,
>   I'm sure it's winter fairly.

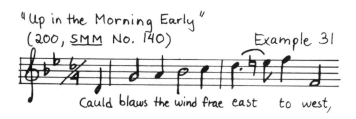

"Up in the Morning Early"
(200, SMM No. 140)   Example 31

Cauld blaws the wind frae east to west,

The tune has a tremendous force which dramatically illustrates the coming and going of the wind and thereby strongly enhances the expression of the song. The melody ascends from G to F^1, covering the whole of the Dorian (minor) mode, and from there it abruptly leaps down by an octave to the lower F. At the top of this melodic curve it receives an extra push down through the dotted rhythm in bar 2, which seems to speed it up (example 31). The tune has a heavy, triple rhythm which expressively brings out words like "blaws", "wind", "loud", and "shill". Other features which help to evoke the scene with the cold wind forcefully sweeping by are the short cut endings of lines 1 and 3, effected by the clipped consonants in "west" and "blast", and the energy of the alliteration in "*d*rift is *d*riving". The chorus has a less bleak expression. It has a sense of humour, its rhythm is lighter with more dotted crotchets and the tune is now major (Ionian), although with a minor twist at the end giving the fourth line a slightly melancholy touch:

> Up in the morning's no for me,
>   Up in the morning early;
> When a' the hills are cover'd wi' snaw,
>   I'm sure it is winter fairly.

"Cauld is the e'enin blast" (601) also sings of the cold wind and the bleak nature in the morning. The song consists of three stanzas set to a tune of three sections (AA^{1}B). The first two stanzas are joined through the similarity of the first lines ("Cauld . . ." and "O cauld . . .") and through the same beginning of the musical phrases (A and A^1). Then there comes an equivocal twist in the third stanza (for B of the tune):

> Ne'er sae murky blew the night
>   That drifted o'er the hill,
> But bonie Peg a Ramsey
>   Gat grist to her mill.

This stanza lies higher and thereby marks the entrance of something new in the song. Kinsley points out that this is Burns's contribution to the tradition of Peggy Ramsay, whose sexual propensities have often been sung of. Burns's song is just a hint, the imagery of milling is often used in bawdry, as Kinsley points out, and the short song ends abruptly and leaves the rest to the listener's imagination.

As we have seen in Chapters 3—6 the majority of Burns's songs deal with love, love as experienced by the lassie, love as seen from the man's point of view, connubial love, and love mingled with nature. Four chapters have been needed to analyse this large group of songs. In the final chapter we shall turn to the other songs, the political songs, the social songs and some miscellaneous songs. They are fewer in number, but most of them are in the best of Burns's lyrical style.

Chapter 7

Social, Political and Miscellaneous Songs

In Burns's production there is also a number of social songs, songs in which he celebrates drinking and dancing and conviviality (here I have also included the masonic songs), and songs in which love is part of social rather than private life. Here the tunes are light and sparkling, the diction simple and easy-flowing, and we can often imagine a group of people joining in the chorus or being gathered round the singer to listen. Most of these songs are written in a traditional and unpretentious style and some of them are actually based on traditional lines.

In "Then Guidwife count the lawin" (346) text and tune combine to convey the conviviality of a pub-scene. The song superbly captures the joy of social drinking and celebrates the enlightening, joining and healing power of ale, brandy and wine. The interior of the pub is depicted as light and cosy, as opposed to the outside which is dark and inhospitable (a common contrast with Burns as pointed out by Kurt Wittig),[1] and by using a metaphor Burns strengthens the effect of this contrast. The drinks are the lights in the night, the whole cosmos is brought into the pub-room, and as Christina Keith points out, the language is "highly imaginative":[2]

Gane is the day and mirk's the night,	*dark*
But we'll ne'er stray for faute o' light,	*lack*
For ale and brandy's stars and moon,	
And blude-red wine's the rysin Sun.	

The implications are of course that the pleasure of gathering together in a pub to drink is so strong that physical darkness is not noticed. The outside is also the place where people "maun fecht and fen" (*must fight and fend*), whereas inside they are "a' in ae accord". Such is the power of drinking that class-differences are levelled out and "ilka man that's drunk's a lord" (*each*). Drinking gives pleasure, and in the last stanza there is displayed an almost Shakespearian joy in this activity with the images of the pool and the trout:

My coggie is a haly pool,	*vessel for liquor*
That heals the wounds o' care and dool;	*misery*
And pleasure is a wanton trout.	
An' ye drink it a', ye'll find him out.	*if*

[1] Kurt Wittig, *The Scottish Tradition in Literature* (Edinburgh: Oliver & Boyd, 1958), p. 207.
[2] Keith, *The Russet Coat,* p. 159.

"Then Guidwife count the lawin'
(346, *SMM* No. 313)

Example 32

Then guidwife count the lawin, the lawin, the lawin,

The pleasure and light-hearted ease which runs through this song is strongly enhanced by the major tune with its assertively rising phrases. It has a lively tempo and a swinging, dotted rhythm, where the heavily marked first and third beats in the first half suggest the rhythmical clapping of hands or the stamping of feet. The tune finely sustains the gaiety and simplicity of the lyric and endows it with a sprightliness which the text itself cannot convey. By turning the poem into a song, the tune also lifts it into the social context which it describes: read the poem and it is about a pub-scene—sing it and we are in the pub, among the people, reliving the situation! The chorus, which Burns had from an old source (*Notes*, p. 55), gives the song a dramatic dimension which is much less noticeable when it is read. The chorus falls on the considerably lower second half of the tune, and through the change of register between the stanzas and the chorus a switch of attention is created. Action is brought into the song, and the scene can be more easily pictured: in the stanzas the men in the pub sing among themselves, maybe gathered round a table, but in the chorus they turn away and call for the landlady and for more drinks: "Then guidwife count the lawin, the lawin, the lawin, / Then guidwife count the lawin, and bring a coggie mair" (*bill*). The repeated "lawin" is fitted to a repeated figure in the tune (example 32) which again evokes that rhythmical clapping of hands or stamping of feet.

A much more droll and humorous situation is conveyed in "Willie brew'd a peck o' maut" (268), a song which also revels in the joy of drinking. It describes a more specific situation, however, than "Then Guidwife count the lawin", which rather has the character of a general, almost universal celebration of ale, brandy and wine. The occasion which gave rise to the creation of this song was the following, as Burns describes it:

M[r] W[m] Nicol, of the High School, Edin[r], during the autumn vacation being at Moffat, honest Allan, who was at that time on a visit to Dalswinton, and I went to pay Nicol a visit. We had such a joyous meeting that M[r] Masterton and I each in our own way should celebrate the business. (*Notes*, p. 52)

The result was a tune, perfect in conveying a state of drunkenness, and a text, which vividly describes the rollicking and merry-making boys. "The song is one of the happiest instances of poetic and musical union in Burns's work", says Kinsley, "the brisk measure, the repetitious phrasing, the lifts and runs—especially in the chorus—catch the mood of 'Bacchanalians' perfectly". There are skips and leaps, ascents and descents, and the tune has a very wide range, but it is particularly the unpredictability of the rhythm, the unexpectedness in the alternation between dotted and undotted notes and snaps which capture the drunken abandon so perfectly. Give the imagination free swing and let the dotted figures stand for the unsteady gait and movements, the undotted for the attempts to seem sober, the snaps for the unexpected loss of balance, or maybe for hiccoughs, and the bacchanalian note of the song cannot be mistaken (examples 33 and 34).

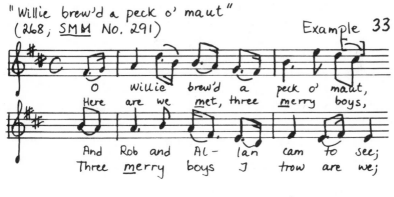

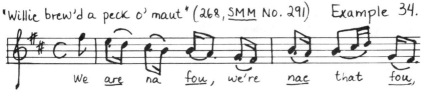

The song describes how Willie, Rob, and Allan get together to brew "a peck o' maut" in the first stanza and how, throughout the course of the song, they get more and more drunk. Yet they strongly claim that they are "na fou" (*drunk*). In the second stanza they have become merrier; there is an indulgence in repetitions, especially of the word "merry", and a happy exuberance in the alliteration on *m*:

> Here are we *met*, three *merry* boys,
>   Three *merry* boys I trow are we;   *believe*
> And *mony* a night we've *merry* been,
>   And *mony mae* we hope to be!   *more*

109

This *m* in "merry" is brought out better when the song is sung, as each time it falls on a long note (example 33). The conviviality heightens and the drunker the men get, the more boastful they become. The moon outside is to guide them home, "But by my sooth she'll wait a wee!" (*little while*), for the drinking is to go on. The man to rise first is a coward and he who falls beside his chair "He is the king amang us three".

The chorus is central, for here lies the declaration of the three men:

> We are na fou, we're nae that fou,
> But just a drappie in our e'e;   *a little liquor*
> The cock may craw, the day may daw,
> And ay we'll taste the barley bree.   *whisky*

This is the drunken man's denial of his state of drunkenness, humorous and ironic, and a "sublime understatement" as Daiches calls it.[3] What is said in the first phrase, "We are na fou, we're nae that fou", is contradicted not only by the obvious attempt to sound convincing (notice the subtle switch of accent from "We *are* na" to the more emphatic "we're *nae*"), but also by the shape of the melody. It descends and ends on snaps for "fou" both times (example 34). This can be taken as the musical illustration of the heads slowly falling down and then being suddenly lifted again with a jerk. In the third line the voices are raised—the melody lies considerably higher here—it rests twice on dotted crotchets ("craw"—"daw"), as if the drunk men cannot say the whole phrase in one go but have to lean on two of the words. Notice also the humorous touch of the effective alliterations in "cock"—"craw" and "day"—"daw" which are very expressive of the drunkard's prattling (see also line 18: "A *c*uckold, *c*oward loun is he!" *fellow*).

Another song which sings the praise of drinking, but also of dancing is "The De'il's awa wi' th' Exciseman" (386). The excise man has been enticed away by the fiddling devil, and as drinks are now free, life can be fully enjoyed again.

"The De'il's awa wi' th' Exciseman"
(386, SMM No. 399)   Example 35.

The deil cam fiddlin thro' the town, And danc'd awa ...

Listen how perfectly Burns has caught the revelling exuberance of the people: "The deil's awa the deil's awa / The deil's awa wi' th' Exciseman" and there is no restraint in the brewing and drinking, dancing and singing. The tune is ma-

[3] Daiches, *Robert Burns*, p. 307.

jor, it lies in the firm and aspiring authentic range and has bold and energetic upward skips. It is a typical jig in swinging 6/8-time and in the first section (for the stanzas) its rhythmic pattern with the heavy first beats (táa-ta-tá-ta-ta) emphasizes the words much more strongly than the mere reading of the poem would do (example 35). This is the heavier part of the dancing, with the stamp of the foot on the first beat, and it is also the part of the song which carries the story. There are repetitions in the stanzas and a profusion of words with cheerful associations of dancing and singing to intensify the sense of merriment and joy. Listen to the second verse with its alliterations, its repetitions, and its rejoicing words:

> We'll mak our maut and we'll brew our drink,
> We'll laugh, sing, and rejoice, man;
> And mony braw thanks to the meikle black deil,   *fine; great*
> That danc'd awa wi' th' Exciseman.

In the chorus, for the second half of the tune, the rhythm lightens, it "gets going", as if everybody dances more excitedly here. The rhythmic pattern is now predominantly tá-ta-ta-tá-ta-ta, with the *d* in "*d*eil" and "*d*anc'd" marking the first beat (example 36):

> The *d*eil's awa the *d*eil's awa
> The *d*eil's awa wi' th' Exciseman,
> He's *d*anc'd awa he's *d*anc'd awa
> He's *d*anc'd awa wi' th' Exciseman.

"The De'il's awa wi' th' Exciseman"
(386, SMM No. 399)   Example 36

The intervals are narrower and this part of the song is therefore more energetic and has a greater intensity. The repetitions in the lyric are varied in the musical context and it is particularly important to notice the climactic lift in the last two-bar phrase (i.e. line 4), which seems to express the relief felt by the people when the exciseman is gone. This is a song of jubilation, of merriment, and of excitement, and the marriage of text and tune calls forth a picture of almost ecstatic dancing and singing.

Two drinking songs have masonic associations (Burns was a freemason from 1781 until his death), "Song" (27) and "The Farewell. To the Brethren of St. James's Lodge, Tarbolton" (115). The first is of an early date and celebrates the "big-belly'd bottle" and the "club of good fellows". The poem is

111

modelled on a popular type of English drinking-song[4] and is set to a major spirited tune which gives the song an extrovert and social character. "The Farewell" is less a drinking-song than a man's party- and parting-song, but its text is too intellectual to be successful for musical setting. It does not allow the listener to participate and to feel the joy of drinking and of being together.

In social life there is not only drinking and dancing and male company, but also women and love-making. In what follows a group of songs will be discussed in which love and the lassies are part of this social life and of the whole scene. The love-songs in the earlier chapters (3—6) speak of serious relations of one man to one woman, they speak of sadness and grief and they speak of parting. They also mirror the joy of love, but they are all private songs where love is depicted as a whole-engulfing experience. The following songs are all sung by men and the love which is presented in them is not part of private so much as of social life. It is love set in a masculine world, a love which causes no smart and which craves no deeper commitment, and a love which is only to be tasted and enjoyed.

In "Green grow the Rashes. A Fragment" (45) no one particular lass but all lassies are praised. The central idea of the song is that the world whirls round the lassies and that the significance of life lies in their creation:

> There's nought but care on ev'ry han',
> In ev'ry hour that passes, O:
> What signifies the life o' man,
> An' 'twere na for the lasses, O.

It is a poem about the way of the world, about the "inevitable, almost cyclical change from lass to lass", as Crawford puts it,[5] about the fugitiveness of worldly riches and the silliness of the man who yet tries to pursue it, and about the wisdom of him who realizes that joy in life is only to be found with the lassies ("The wisest Man the warl' saw, / He dearly lov'd the lasses, O"). There is a mixture of optimism and joy with a sense of mutability and with the shortness of life in the song. The tune is sparkling and it strengthens the optimistic note in the text. It is major, assertive in the authentic range and four-beat rhythm, and it has phrases which rise by skips of thirds, fourths and fifths. But it ends in the minor, and this somehow seems to recall the transience of life implied in the lyric. The chorus sings of the lassies and sums up the philosophy of the song:

> *Green grow the rashes, O;*
> *Green grow the rashes, O;*
> *The sweetest hours that e'er I spend,*
> *Are spent among the lasses, O.*[6]

[4] H-H, I, p. 417.
[5] Crawford, p. 282.
[6] The whole stanza is italicized in Kinsley.

112

It lies higher than the stanzas, has more boldly rising skips and is therefore more extrovert in the display of gaiety, in spite of that strange minor close.

"Song" (312, for the tune, see 84:208) is also a praise of women, but it strikes a somewhat different note: though women's minds may turn and shift like winter winds, their company and love is yet worth enjoying. The tune is major and dotted and the happy abandon of the chorus (which was old, see *Notes*, p. 52) raises the song to a universal level:

> For a' that, an' a' that,
>   An' twice as meikel's a' that,   *much*
> My dearest bluid to do them guid,
>   They're welcome till 't for a' that.

The song points to no personal attachments, it talks of the women as "they", and it is the joy of loving them which is emphasized.

"O May thy morn" (576) takes us back to the pub-scene and as Kinsley notes, love and conviviality are here finely fused within the same song. Love-making is connected with wine-drinking, and love and social life receive the same attention in the song (see for instance the collocation of wine and love in lines 3—4 below). The situation is this: the men are gathered in the pub. One of them remembers an affair with a sweet lassie and gets carried away by the thought of her:

> O May, thy morn was ne'er sae sweet,
>   As the mirk night o' December;   *dark*
> For sparkling was the rosy wine,
>   And private was the chamber:
> And dear was she, I dare na name,
>   But I will ay remember.—
> And dear was she, I dare na name,
>   But I will ay remember.—

He then turns to his friends in the more extrovert second stanza and love is now seen in perspective. There is a toast for those who drink ("And here's to them, that, like oursel, / Can push about the jorum" *drinking-vessel*), and there is a toast for the lassies ("And here's to them, we dare na tell, / The dearest o' the quorum"), and love has received a place in the whole social context. The tune is major, but has a minor ending, descending phrases in the first half, a slow tempo, and a smooth flow of undotted notes which seem to strengthen the nostalgic quality of the lyric. For the second half of each stanza the expression intensifies: the tune now lifts and the singer excitedly praises the lassie he will never forget (stanza 1, see above) and the lassies in general (stanza 2).

"My love she's but a lassie yet" (293) also takes place in the pub, where a man tells his drinking-friends about his lassie with rather mixed feelings. He regrets the day he sought her, for she was impertinent and despised him because of his poverty, and he now turns to his drink and his male company for comfort:

> Come draw a drap o' the best o't yet,
> Come draw a drap o' the best o't yet:
> Gae seek for Pleasure whare ye will,
> But here I never misst it yet.—

This again is love in a social context as seen in the perspective of the masculine world. The major light-tripping reel-tune with its octave skips and shifts between the high and low register precludes any sentimental or sad overtones and it gives the song the character of a passing affair among many. Or as Crawford puts it in his fine analysis of the song: "The elements of the little drama are subordinated to the rhythms of the original dance, and we feel that 'this is the way the world wags,' in endless, light-hearted movement, and that passions and disappointments, as well as 'mirth an' dancin',' have their place in the *perpetuum mobile*."[7]

In "Theniel Menzies' bony Mary" (177) a girl is praised by all the young men ("We drank a health to bonie Mary") and the song places her in a social, rather than private, context. There is a connection between loving, drinking, dancing, and playing, and he who kisses "bonie Mary" must also dance with her as part of the game. In the chorus we can almost hear the men join in the praise of the girl. The onset is emphatic as the tune lacks the upbeat here, and the melody swings rhythmically and joyfully up and down for the first two lines, expressing the communal singing and the playfulness of the scene:

> Theniel Menzies' bonie Mary,
> Theniel Menzies' bonie Mary,
> Charlie Grigor tint his plaidie   *lost; cloak*
> Kissin Theniel's bonie Mary.—

The tune has a lively and sinewy vitality and a rhytmical swing which suits the poetical theme of rollicking, social joy very well. There is a steady mark of the tempo-beat through the snaps and the dotted quavers which accentuates the energetic character of the lyric. There is energy in the two-syllable words on the snaps ("tarry", "kissin", "haffet", "berry" etc.), in the one-syllable words on the dotted quavers (e.g. "brig", "blink", "lads", "gat"), and in the alliterations and internal rhymes of stanza 2 (see below). Also the unexpected turns in the melody and the major quality of the tune capture the gaiety of the scene very well. There is a sudden change of direction at the end of B in the tune (its form is ABCB[1]) which has a fine dramatic effect, particularly in the second and third stanzas. In the second bonie Mary is described:

---

[7] Crawford, p. 278.

114

A	Her een sae bright, her brow sae white,	
	Her haffet locks as brown's a berry;	*temple*
B	And ay they dimpl't wi' a smile,	
	The rosy cheeks o' bonie Mary.—	

Here the first two lines are only descriptive and the musical phrases suitably descending. With the turn of direction and the change of register in the tune (it abruptly leaps up an octave to ascend to the highest point of the tune, see example 37) something happens in the poem too. It brightens up, the cheeks "dimpl't wi' a smile", and the music seems to illustrate the joy of the man who sings it. In the last stanza the strathspey-rhythm of the tune becomes the true accompaniment of the dance:

A	We lap and danc'd the lee-lang day,	*leapt; live long*
	Till Piper lads were wae and weary;	
B	But Charlie gat the spring to pay	*dance*
	For kissin Theniel's bonie Mary.—	

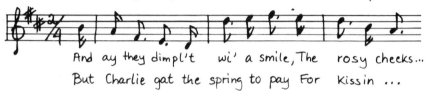

"Theniel Menzies' bony Mary" (177, SMM No. 156)   Example 37

And ay they dimpl't wi' a smile, The rosy cheeks...
But Charlie gat the spring to pay For kissin ...

When the tune leaps up (example 37) Charlie gets "the spring to pay" and the dramatic and climactic effect of that line can hardly be conveyed if the song is not sung.

Before turning to the political songs, two comical songs should be briefly mentioned in which love and love-making lie behind the humorous themes. "Scroggam" (595) is short and the humour works by implication. The situation is given in six lines only, and the rest of each stanza is filled out by a refrain. The second stanza tells us that "The gudewife's dochter fell in a fever" and that "The priest o' the parish fell in anither". This is how it ends:

They laid the twa i' the bed thegither,	
Scroggam;	
That the heat o' the tane might cool the tither,	*one ... other*
Sing auld Cowl, lay you down by me,	
Scroggam, my Dearie, ruffum.	

The first line of each stanza which sings slowly to a rising melodic line is effectively cut short by the nonsensical word "Scroggam", falling on a low snap, followed by a pause. This pause has a strong dramatic effect for it makes us wonder what will follow. The music of the third line strives even higher but is interrupted in a similar way, although now by the two-line refrain: enough has been said for the listener to be able to grasp the situation, and he can join in the chorus and share the fun!

In "We'll hide the Couper behint the door" (564), as Crawford aptly puts it, "overtones of cruelty and contempt for the village cuckold are swept away by the fantasy, which is generated as much by the irresistible motion of its grand old tune, *Bab at the bowster,* as by the dance of the words themselves".[8] The assertively rising phrases of the tune, its emphatic lifts and the dancing 6/8-rhythm enhance the cheerful quality of the poem. Through the phrasal repetitions in the lyric (e.g. in stanza 1: "He sought them out, he sought them in, / Wi', deil hae her! and, deil hae him!") and through the chorus, where the people seem to join in and make fun of the couper behind his back, the movement, the playfulness and the exuberance of the scene are effectively conveyed (in this the song reminds one very much of "The De'il's awa wi' th' Exciseman", see above).

In Burns's output there are also a fairly large number of political and patriotic songs, songs which grew out of Burns's ardent interest in the politics and history of Scotland, but also out of a vivid tradition. The Jacobite movement[9] had a central significance in Scottish folk-song (something of which James Hogg's collection of *Jacobite Relics of Scotland*[10] bear evidence) and although its political force ceased after the rebellions in 1715 and 1745, the poetic tradition lingered for a long time after. As Daiches points out, Burns realized the importance of perpetuating the folk emotion inherent in this tradition,[11] and he collected, refurbished, and wrote new songs with great enthusiasm. Songs which had texts with politically unacceptable material he gave a new, inoffensive wording in order to preserve Jacobite tunes.

In some of these songs the tunes seem to take second place to the narration or message and only give the text a general sense of strength and vigour. This is the case with "A Fragment" (38, for Burns's first choice of tune, see "Killicrankie", 313), an early song which gives a sketchy account of the

[8] Crawford, p. 323.

[9] The Jacobites were the supporters of the Stuart King James II, who fled to France after the Glorious Revolution in 1688, and his descendants, of which Prince Charles Edward, Bonie Prince Charles, is best known in the songs. For an introduction to the songs of the Jacobite movement and their historical background, see William Gunnyon, *Illustrations of Scottish History, Life and Superstition from Song and Ballad* (Glasgow: Robert Forrester, 1879), pp. 115—140.

[10] James Hogg, ed., *The Jacobite Relics of Scotland: being songs, airs, and legends of the adherents of the House of Stuart,* 2 vols. (Edinburgh: W. Blackwood, 1819—21).

[11] Daiches, "Robert Burns and Jacobite Song", p. 137.

American War of Independence from the Boston Tea Party in 1773 to the election victory of William Pitt in 1784. It is a long song, crammed with names and historical details in which any textual-melodic subtleties would be lost on the listener. The tune is an energetic reel associated with many Jacobite songs. Later (as "Killicrankie" had already been used in *SMM*) Burns changed it to "The Earl of Glencairn's", a tune which, in Kinsley's view, is "equally suited, despite the shift into strathspey rhythm, to the rhyme-scheme of his poem". "The Dumfries Volunteers" (484), a patriotic song written for the Dumfries volunteers at the threat of a French invasion in the spring of 1795, is shorter and more concise. Here too, the text is the most important, although the song would lose much of its encouraging character without the tune, which, with its undotted rhythm, major mode and assertively rising phrases lifts the poem to a more extrovert level.

"Nithsdale's welcome hame" (279) commemorates the rebuilding of a family mansion called Terreagles, but has political overtones (William Maxwell, fifth Earl of Nithsdale and the grandfather of Lady Winifred, who began the restoration of the building, took part in the Jacobite Rebellion in 1715, was sentenced to death, but managed to escape). The poem is set to a slow tune with dotted rhythm which endows the song with grandeur, mightiness and effective tension. There is a sudden change of register in bar 3, which gives the third line of each stanza a dramatic expression, which would be lost in a read version. The import of the song is weakened, however, through the repetition of the last half-stanza to cover the tune.

"Awa whigs awa" (303) is a more concise and therefore much more effective Jacobite song. It describes the destruction brought about by the Whigs[12] ("The whigs cam o'er us for a curse, / And we hae done wi' thriving"), and in the chorus (which was old, as Kinsley points out) the long-felt discontent with the present state is expressed in forceful and threatening shouts:

> Awa whigs awa,
> Awa whigs awa,
> Ye're but a pack o' traitor louns,   *rascal*
> Ye'll do nae gude at a'.

When sung, the impact of these menacing shouts is considerably heightened. The tune rises from the third note to the fifth of the scale for the first line, and then with heightened intensity, from the third to the sixth for the second. As it falls on a crotchet, the second syllable of "awa" is effectively prolonged as in loud shouting (example 38). The second half of the tune is an elaboration of the

---

[12] The Whigs were the opponents of the Jacobites and claimed the right to exclude the heir from the throne. The term also denoted Scottish Presbyterianism, Nonconformity and rebellion.

first with the same emphatic rises. It is more animated, however, because of the semi-quaver figures and herein lies the contrast between the chorus and the stanzas. The former is very tight and tense. It has an expression of held-back threat and is directed straight at the Whigs, whereas the stanzas are narrative and give the background.

"Awa whigs awa" (303, SMM No. 263)   Example 38

The first stanza is the most striking with its image of the blooming roses and thistles which withered when the Whigs came. These images are juxtaposed through the alliteration in "*flourish'd fresh* and *fair*" and "*frost* in June" and the contrast is emphasized through the shift in the music: for the first two lines the melodic direction is upward, enhancing the optimism which is embodied in them, whereas in the last two it is downward. Notice also the "but" on a top note, which also marks the change of expression:

> Our thrissles flourish'd fresh and fair,   *thistle*
> And bonie bloom'd our roses;
> *But* whigs cam like a frost in June,
> And wither'd a' our posies.

The following stanzas tell of the "sad decay in church and state" caused by the Whigs, and show indignation at the fact that "Grim Vengeance lang has taen a nap". This is a song which is meant to encourage, and it successfully does so through simple diction, striking images, verbal music and by making maximum use of the inherent expressive possibilities of the tune.

"Killiecrankie" (313) tells of the Battle of Killiecrankie in vigorous language and to a vigorous tune. This battle was fought in 1689 between the forces of James VII, led by Graham of Claverhouse (Viscount Dundee) and the Dutch-English royal troops under General Hugh Mackay. The royal troops were put to flight, but Dundee fell in the moment of victory. The song has a dialogue-form and the answer is given by one of Mackay's men who luckily survived, in pursuit, because Pitcur fell in a ditch ("An' Clavers gat a clankie" *blow*). The poem has a simple diction and there are effective repetitions of phrases (e.g. "I faught at land, I faught at sea, / At hame I faught my Auntie, O"), internal rhymes and alliterations (e.g. "The bauld Pit*cur f*ell in a *furr*, / An' *C*lavers gat a *c*lankie, O" *bold; deep ditch*). When sustained by the major tune with its

118

energetic rising phrases and undotted duple rhythm the song has a fine martial impact and the message in the chorus seems delivered with pathos:

> An ye had been whare I hae been,
> Ye wad na been sae cantie O;   *cheerful*
> An ye had seen what I hae seen,
> I' th' braes o' Killiecrankie O.   *hills*

"O Kenmure's on and awa, Willie" (364) is another song which takes up an historical event in a spirited, but more relaxed manner. Some men have gathered to praise Kenmure in song and in drink, Kenmure who was commander of the rebel forces in the south of Scotland and raised the Jacobite standard in Lochmaben in 1715, but who was beheaded when taken prisoner by the English. Here also the language is simple, largely depending on repetitions, it is well suited to communal singing ("Here's Kenmure's health in wine, Willie, / Here's Kenmure's health in wine"), and the major tune has a light-hearted and energetic swing in triple rhythm which endows the song with an extrovert and exciting character.

The patriotic song above all others is "Robert Bruce's March to Bannockburn" (425, for the tune, see "Hey tuti tatey", 206) which, with its national pathos and pathos of freedom has become one of Burns's most popular. It is *the* song about the Scottish war of independence, and Burns gives the following account of its creation:

I do not know whether the old air, "Hey tutti taitie," may rank among this number; but well I know that, with Fraser's Hautboy, it has often filled my eyes with tears.—There is a tradition, which I have met with in many places of Scotland, that it was Robert Bruce's March at the battle of Bannock-burn.—This thought, in my yesternight's evening walk, warmed me to a pitch of enthusiasm on the theme of Liberty & Independance, which I threw into a kind of Scots Ode, fitted to the Air, that one might suppose to be the gallant ROYAL SCOT'S address to his heroic followers on that eventful morning.—(Letter 582)

It is set to a tune of both simplicity and strength without which the poem would lose a great deal of its power.[13] Even the priggish George Thomson finally realized that this was the only tune which could do the poem justice. He was first of all opposed to Burns's choice of tune and wanted him to accept another one ("Lewie Gordon"), and he even suggested changes in the poem to accom-

---

[13] The song was printed in both *SMM* (No. 170) and *SC* (1803, No. 133). In *SMM*, however, it is not coupled to its prescribed tune as that tune had already been printed with "Hey tuti tatey". In his comment to the song, Kinsley says that the two parts of the tune have to be transposed for 425. That is how the tune was printed in *SC*, but Burns himself referred Thomson to "Clarke's set of the tune" in *SMM* (Letter 582). There the high part is printed first, as it is also in *CPC* (1751, III, No. 13), which Burns certainly knew. The arrangement of the tune which will be considered here is therefore that of *SMM*.

modate it to the rhythm of that tune, changes which Burns objected to as he found they would make his song too tame. On reconsideration, however, Thomson changed his mind and in a note in *SC* he remarks: "The Editor, however, having since examined the Air '*Hey tutti taiti*' with more particular attention, frankly owns that he has changed his opinion, and that he thinks it much better adapted for giving energy to the Poetry" (quoted by Kinsley, II, p. 707).

The song arouses patriotic feelings and its dominating expression is that of power and energy. The tight-knit structure is important, for it keeps the strong emotional forces within bounds and thereby endows the song with a tremendous tension. Each stanza is held together by a binding-rhyme and all the six stanzas by the common rhyme of the fourth lines (aaab/cccb/dddb etc.), and furthermore the beginnings of the lines are united through a common word ("Scots", "see", "wha", "free-", "by"). The form of the tune is AB, where A_4 and B_4 are the same and therefore correspond to the fourth lines (with the b-rhyme) of each stanza.

The song opens by attack with the exhorting lines:

> Scots, wha hae wi' WALLACE bled,
> Scots, wham BRUCE has aften led,
> Welcome to your gory bed,—
> Or to victorie.—

The first half of the tune (A) starts in the high register and has no upbeat, so that the force and intensity of the important opening word, "Scots", is tremendous. The rhythm is quadruple and dotted and this in combination with the rising melodic lines gives the tune its tension and energy (example 39). With the dotted repetition of one note in the first bar followed by the skip up by a third, the opening line recalls an arousing bugle call. The exhortations of the first two lines lead up to a climax in the third, where the melodic line starts high (on "Welcome") and then descends (bar 3 in example 39). The major quality of the pentatonic tune should be noticed as it gives the song a sense of optimism.

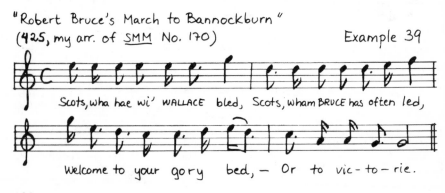

"Robert Bruce's March to Bannockburn"
(425, my arr. of SMM No. 170)   Example 39

Scots, wha hae wi' WALLACE bled, Scots, wham BRUCE has often led,

Welcome to your gory bed, — Or to vic-to-rie.

The second stanza (for B of the tune) starts low with the threatening words "Now's the day, and now's the hour" and then works itself up to a stronger intensity in the third line, where the tune lies higher. Through the whole song there is a shift of expression from the high register in stanzas 1, 3 and 5 to the low in stanzas 2, 4 and 6. The high start in bar 3 is particularly effective in stanza 5, where "We" is accented through the top note and so takes on a significance which is lost in a read version. When Daiches complains that the song is "essentially a rhetorical poem of slogans and exhortations"[14] he talks about the poetry only and forgets its relation to the music. When carried by the tune the repetitions and antitheses and other rhetorical devices are varied and given an emotional dimension of pathos without which the impact of this eighteenth-century camp song is considerably weakened.

Other patriotic songs are melancholy. "Such a parcel of rogues in a nation" (375) speaks the words of nostalgia, of sadness, and of love for Scotland. It exposes the opposition between then and now, between the old time of the "ancient glory" (and "glory" is emphasized through a long dotted crotchet in a cadence) and the present state of involuntary Union with England. It has a development from a sense of loss and acceptance of the new state (lines 1—4) to a declaration of refusal and protest in the last half-stanza of the song (for the high part of the tune):

> But pith and power, till my last hour,
> I'll mak this declaration;
> We're bought and sold for English gold,
> Such a parcel of rogues in a nation!

There is a melancholy in the first part of the tune (constituted by the slow tempo, the minor mode, the low register, the undulating melodic lines and the plagal range), which is particularly expressive for the first half-stanza with its repeated "Farewell". Against this is set the second part, which is high and major, has boldly rising phrases and snaps, and lies in the steady authentic range. This section embodies the national pathos, the painful knowledge of the present (see the emphatic "now" in line 5), the valour and the protest. The tune thus endows the poem with an emotional dimension which is lost if the poem is only read. The inner tensions, the pride and the anger as well as the melancholy and sadness can only be fully heard and felt if the song is sung.

Of the political songs "There'll never be peace till Jamie comes hame" (326) is the most tragic and nostalgic. Here again the subject matter is that of Scotland after the Union, but in this song it is viewed from a more personal level. In a desolate setting an old man sings about the tragedy which has afflicted his family:

---

[14] Daiches, *Robert Burns,* p. 308.

> By yon castle wa' at the close of the day,
> I heard a man sing tho' his head it was grey;
> And as he was singing the tears down came,
> There'll never be peace till Jamie comes hame.—

This song, also, depends on its tune to convey the emotions behind the man's words. Its three-beat lilt and slow tempo finely express the resignation of the old man and give the song a sense of nostalgia which the poem itself cannot convey so strongly. It is sombre and melancholy and the minor mode with its open ending has a strange indefinite character which seems to intensify the gloom of the scene. The form is ABCB, where B is a variation of A, ending one degree higher and preparing for the climax on the high ascent in C. Burns has effectively used this ascent for a corresponding poetical intensification in lines 3, 7, 11, and 15, which become dramatic outbursts of grief when sung. After that, with the return to B, the refrain functions as a relief ("There'll never be peace" etc.). In the last stanza, however, the old man shows a spark of protest and anger, and the lift in C now becomes an outburst of protest:

> Now life is a burden that bows me down,
> Sin I tint my bairns, and he tint his crown;   *lost; children*
> But till my last moments my words are the same,
> There'll never be peace till Jamie comes hame.—

Another song which tells of war from a personal point of view is "Orananaoig, or, The Song of death" (330). The title of the song is that of the Gaelic tune to which it is set, and it inspired Burns to write a poem about death as it is experienced by the soldier. The song exposes an opposition between life and death and between the coward and the brave. The first half-stanza is a farewell to everything that is light and gay in life, expressed through words with pleasant associations like "fair", "green", "gay", "loves and friendships", "dear tender". The same tune is repeated twice (AA^1), suggesting a similar structure of the lines:

> A   Farewell, thou fair day; thou green earth; and ye skies,
>   Now gay with the broad setting sun!
> A^1 Farewell, loves and friendships, ye dear tender ties!
>   Our race of existence is run.

With the lift and the rising phrases in B, death is addressed ("Thou grim king of terrors") and the mood changes from light to dark and gloomy. If the first half is passively yielding to death on arched musical phrases, the second is actively braving it and the snaps on "coward" and "terrors" emphasize its bold quality. The rhetoric also of the second stanza follows the pattern of the music with the repeated "Thou strik'st", and in the last four lines the rising melodic phrases intensify the glorification of the brave soldier, who does not shun death in the

122

fight for "Our king and our Country". Burns has not, however, succeeded very well in adapting the words to the tune in this song. In the second line, for instance, the preposition "with" is clumsily set on the top of a melodic contour. The second syllable of "setting" in the same line, "a" in line 10 and "the" in line 16 also receive unnecessary accents through the sudden tonal leap down and through the fact that the setting is semi-syllabic at this point ("sett-i-ing", "a-a", and "the-e").

A similarly gloomy creation is the strange "Song" (555) called "A Lassie all alone. Recitative" in *SMM* (No. 405). It is a song with a midnight setting where all is silence ("The winds were laid, the air was still") and the only sound that can be heard comes from the burn in the distance. In this atmosphere a lassie moans in the chorus "Lamenting our lads beyond the sea; / In the bluidy wars they fa', and our honor's gane and a'", and in a true romantic fashion also a ghost appears, wailing and weeping: "And frae his harp sic strains did flow, / Might rous'd the slumbering Dead to hear". As the title in *SMM* implies the tune is extremely monotonous and recitative-like (it led Stephen Clarke to believe that it was "an old Chant of the ROMISH CHURCH", Letter 637) and is therefore a perfect accompaniment of the desolate poem. Crawford who has analysed the political aspects of this song suggests that the war referred to is the contemporary struggle with France.[15]

Three songs connect politics and patriotism with love, songs in which the singers are all women. In "The Highland widow's lament" (590) the poor widow tells her tragic life story, how she used to be rich and happy, how the battle at Culloden in 1745 took her Donald from her and how "Nae woman in the warld wide / Sae wretched now as me." It is a song of deep grief, but also of protest against injustices:

> Their waefu' fate what need I tell,
> Right to the wrang did yield;
> My Donald and his Country fell
> Upon Culloden field.—

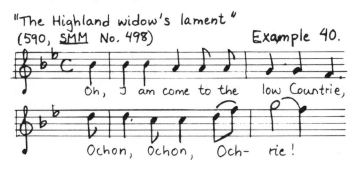

"The Highland widow's lament"
(590, SMM No. 498)   Example 40.

Oh, I am come to the low Countrie,
Ochon, Ochon, Och- rie!

[15] Crawford, pp. 244—45.

The tune has a wide emotional range embodying both resignation and indignation in its very slow tempo, minor mode and melodic curves. The first two-bar phrase (a) is falling, expressing passive sadness for the first line of each stanza. Then follows a dramatic outburst of grief which is very incisive with the refrain in stanzas 1–4 ("Ochon, Ochon, Ochrie", see example 40). The climax comes in the high section of c (for line 3 of each stanza) before the tune resumes a sense of resignation in d.

"O'er the water to Charlie" (211, for the tune, see 128) is a lighter and more uncomplicated song. The political theme (the restoration of Bonny Prince Charlie) is here expressed through the words of a girl longing for her lover, a common way of concealing the Jacobite character of a song (cf. above Ch. 3, n. 13), and as Daiches points out the song "captures with complete success the personal and 'occasional' nature of much Jacobite folk-song".[16] The stanzas are the expression of the girl's love ("Come boat me o'er, come row me o'er, / Come boat me o'er to Charlie"), whereas in the chorus other singers join in and the political subject is more outspoken:

> We'll o'er the water, we'll o'er the sea,
>   We'll o'er the water to Charlie;
> Come weal, come woe, we'll gather and go,
>   And live or die wi' Charlie.—

The tune is simple and gay with a 6/8 jig-rhythm and a major mode which enhances this "occasional" and light-hearted nature of the song.

"The young Highland Rover" (176) conceals the same political theme under the cover of a young lassie's love-song. This song, however, is not as light and cheerful as "O'er the water to Charlie". The girl's sadness is conveyed through a slow and melancholy tune with a wide range and expressive upward leaps. It is also mirrored in the cold and gloomy landscape:

> Loud blaw the frosty breezes,
>   The snaws the mountains cover;
> Like winter on me seizes
>   Since my young Highland rover
> Far wanders nations over.

The second stanza expresses hope, and the reawakening of nature becomes symbolic of the expected return of the Highland rover (i.e. Prince Charles Edward). However, the minor tune gives the girl's words an undertone of pessimism. The sudden switch from despondency in the first stanza to joy in the second is counteracted by the tune, and the dominant expression of the song therefore remains sad.

[16] Daiches, "Robert Burns and Jacobite Song", p. 148.

124

"The Captain's Lady" (296) is only loosely connected with politics. War is here the background, and when the lover comes back from it, "To the shades we'll go / And in love enjoy it". The tune is light and major and has a marching character with quick semi-quavers, which become expressive of the beating drums and rattling cannons in the first stanza:

> O mount and go,
> Mount and make you ready,
> O mount and go,
> And be the Captain's Lady.

There now remain five odd songs which do not belong to any of the groups already discussed. In "McPherson's Farewell" (196) Burns shows how he could turn a narrative broadside ballad[17] into an excellent, lyric song. Instead of telling the story about McPherson, thief and murderer, as the old ballad does, he concentrates upon one single aspect—that of McPherson's bold and revengeful spirit when facing death. The old ballad gives an outline of McPherson's life, explains why he had to be hanged and shows how this courageous hero still feared hell ("But yet Hell's torments I do fear / When once my life is gone"). There is a moral in it ("According to the life ye lead, / Rewarded ye shall be") and a sense of atonement, something which, as Thornton points out, Burns has got rid of in his song.[18] " 'McPherson's Farewel,' is mine, excepting the chorus, & one stanza", Burns says to Thomson in a letter (Letter 644) and, as Kinsley suggests, the following stanza in the old ballad probably gave him a hint for his chorus:

> Then wantonly and rantingly
> I am resolv'd to die;
> And with undaunted courage I
> Shall mount this fatal tree.

There is an important difference between the ballad and the song, however, for Burns uses the idea of McPherson's dauntless spirit in a chorus which is to be sung throughout the whole song. As such it becomes a constant reminder of his courage, whereas in the ballad it is a conclusion which is reached at the end.

There is no development of McPherson's character in Burns's song, but the first stanza plunges straight into his feelings when he is waiting for death by the gallows-tree. The song is very much "here and now" and the only flash-back on his life is given in stanza 4:

---

[17] One version of the old ballad is to be found in James Maidment, ed., *Scotish Songs and Ballads* (Edinburgh: T. G. Stevenson, 1859), pp. 29—34, another, defective one in Herd, *The Ancient and Modern Scots Songs,* I, pp. 99—101. The quoted lines are given from Maidment, pp. 33—34.

[18] Thornton, *The Tuneful Flame,* p. 13.

I've liv'd a life of sturt and strife;   *contention*
    I die by treacherie:
It burns my heart I must depart
    And not avenged be.

Tradition has it that McPherson composed this tune for the fiddle and played it
on his way to the gallows-tree, a tradition of which, as Kinsley points out,
Burns makes fine use in his own song. With masterly skill he sets the chorus on
the high part of the tune as against the stanzas on the low with a dramatic, but
also humorous effect. The high part of the tune has a reel-like quality with its
undotted notes, its runs of semi-quavers, its steady rhythm and with its skips
between the first and fifth of the tune, so typical of fiddle-music. It lies steady
within the authentic range of the mode and it has a clear major feel. All this
makes the chorus seem more extrovert and more defiant than the stanzas,
which lie on the low, first half of the tune. In the chorus McPherson's bold
spirit is displayed with a grim humour, whereas the stanzas are more reflective
(see e.g. line 9: "O what is death but parting breath?") and more complex. The
range of the low part of the tune is plagal, its contour is undulating and descending, and its expression is consequently more passive than the second half.
The contrast between the chorus and the stanzas does not only mirror
McPherson's character but also reflects the scene: the chorus becomes the objective comment on the situation, as in a Greek drama. The people who stand
by the gallows-tree, waiting to see the murderer hanged, sing:

Sae rantingly, sae wantonly,   *merrily*
    Sae dauntingly gae'd he:
He play'd a spring, and danc'd it round
    Below the gallows-tree.

The personal pronoun of the chorus is "he", whereas in the stanzas it is "I".
McPherson himself sings in the stanzas, he then takes up his fiddle (cf. the
tradition) and plays the rant to which the people sing about his boldness—this
is how one can picture the scene.

With a sensitive ear Burns has moulded his verses on the musical phrasing.
Each two-bar phrase takes two lines of the stanza, which are thought-
contained units. This arrangement of the verses is necessary as the cadence in
bar 2 is very clear. The singer will rest here, take a breath and go on to the next
two-bar phrase. The second stanza is less successful in this respect. Here only
the *first* line forms the first unit, and the last *three* the second, and the two sections are separated by a question-mark. This arrangement stands in direct opposition to the natural musical phrasing, and when sung the meaning becomes
confused: "O what is death but parting breath on many a bloody plain" (first
musical phrase) and "I've dar'd his face, and in this place I scorn him yet

126

again" (second musical phrase). In its printed version the meaning of the stanza is clearer:

> O what is death but parting breath?
>   On many a bloody plain
> I've dar'd his face, and in this place
>   I scorn him yet again!

Songs about young girls or women are to be found in profusion in Burns's production, whereas songs about boys or men are rare. "There's a youth in this City" (300) and "Sandy and Jockie" (309) are two such songs. The first is about a laddie who spited all girls because he loved himself "dearest of a' ". It is set to a melancholy tune, not quite corresponding to the expression of the poem, which has a matter-of-fact tone and a touch of humour. "Sandy and Jockie" sings about two boys, one rich and unhappy, the other poor but happy. Burns got the inspiration for the song from a couplet by D'Urfey which he used as the starting-point to his own song:[19] "Twa bony lads were Sandy and Jockie; / Jockie was lo'ed but Sandy unlucky". He has not quite managed to make an organic whole of D'Urfey's lines and his own, however, and there is a discrepancy between the quoted couplet and the rest of the song. Burns proceeds to describe Jockie as the "laird" with plenty of land and money and Sandy as the "king o' gude fellows" but with no riches. Jockie marries for money and Sandy for love, "So Jockie had siller, and Sandy had pleasure". If this line is compared to the second of D'Urfey's the switch is obvious: the antithesis between Jockie and Sandy remains, but in Burns's lines the roles are reversed, and there is a *moral* in it—he who marries for money can never be happy. Nor does the poem very well catch the expression of the tune, which is a lament. The latter lacks the simplicity needed to bring out the antitheses between the two boys in lines 3—6 ("Jockie"—"But Sandie", "Jockie"—"And Sandie") and it seems too pretentious a tune for the rather simple poem.

Two love-songs tell of love and courting from the narrator's point of view (cf. Chs. 3 and 4), "Duncan Davison" (202, for the tune, see 30) and "On a bank of Flowers" (292). Both are humorous songs, although "Duncan Davison" more overtly so, and both are about the ardent wooer who is refused by the girl but at the end of the song finally accepted. In "Duncan Davison" the shift from the girl's disdainfulness to her acceptance of the boy is drastic and straightforward, whereas in "On a bank of Flowers" it is only just hinted at.

The first half-stanza of "Duncan Davison", which is based on an old bawdy song (see Kinsley), is the introduction to the story and the presentation of the boy and the girl (notice the repeated "there was"):

---

[19] Dick, *The Songs*, p. 490.

> There was a lass, they ca'd her Meg,
>   And she held o'er the moors to spin;
> There was a lad that follow'd her,
>   They ca'd him Duncan Davison.

These lines suitably lie on the low part of the tune (A), which is firmly anchored round the tonic. This is repeated three times on heavy beats, and the rhythm of this section is dotted. In the second half (B) the tune lies one octave higher (it lifts already in A_4, see example 41), its rhythm is lighter, it dances and swings and is more like a reel. The melody is more active with its emphatic runs up and it is now centred round the fifth note of the scale. After the presentation of characters, and responding to the change of expression in the tune, the attention in the second half-stanza is focused on scenery and on action. There is a confrontation between Meg and Duncan, he tries to win her attention, but she is only irritated with him (notice how the alliterations in lines 5 and 7, accented as they fall on heavy beats in the tune, give added emphasis to the expression):

> The *moor* was driegh, and *M*eg was skiegh,   *dreary; proud*
>   Her favour Duncan could na win;
> For *wi*' the rock she *w*ad him knock,   *distaff*
>   And ay she shook the temper-pin.   *screw for regulating the*
>   *movement of the spinning-wheel*

"Duncan Davison' (202, SMM No. 149)   Example 41.

Upon the banks they eas'd their shanks, And ay she set the wheel between:

In the second stanza Burns has more skilfully taken advantage of the contrast between the two sections of the tune to express the dramatic development of the story. The first three lines (for the low part of the tune) are descriptive. There are no conflicts and no sense of either acceptance or refusal and the scene is all pleasantness with words like "lightly", "clear", "green", and "eas'd". Then, in the fourth line and on the lift in A_4 something happens which prepares for the little drama in the second half: "Upon the banks they eas'd their shanks, / *And ay she set the wheel between*". For a reader this line will pass almost unnoticed, but when delivered on the emphatic lift in the tune (example 41) it becomes dramatic and illustrative of the suddenness of the action. The climax of the song follows in the next four lines:

> But Duncan swoor a haly aith
>   That Meg should be a bride the morn,
> Then Meg took up her spinning-graith,   *tools*
>   And flang them a' out o'er the burn.   *stream*

The scene is all calmness at first and Duncan and Meg are sitting down to rest in the beautiful scenery. Then Meg will not have Duncan sit close to her and she puts the spinning-wheel between them. Duncan excitedly stands up, swears he will win her, Meg suddenly "sees" him, flings the wheel in the burn and embraces him. This is a free interpretation of the scene as it appears, when both text and tune are considered.

In the last stanza the lovers are united and they plan for a life together. There is an emphasis on "we", the word is repeated three times on heavy beats and the first "we" is very emphatic as that bar lacks an upbeat. The fourth line "When ye set by the wheel at e'en" echoes the role of the spinning-wheel in the second stanza. Kinsley points out that the last half-stanza is not wholly by Burns, but taken from a fragment in Herd. It is not thematically connected with the rest of the song, but serves well as a comment on it. The first stanza was an exposition, introducing the two characters, the second was the development of the story and the last, finally, the recapitulation, where the two lovers are reconciled and joined. The story about Meg's refusal and acceptance of Duncan Davison is told with humour, and the gaiety of the tune forces the listener into a detached attitude at the same time as it makes him understand the feelings and intensity behind the action.

In "On a bank of Flowers" (292) we find a similar situation in a pastoral setting and in a pastoral style. But beneath the surface of this rather conventional rococo-painting of "the youthful blooming Nelly", desired and followed by Willy, there are touches of humour and irony in both text and tune which suggest that Burns did not mean this song to be wholly serious. The first half of the tune (AA) is devoted to the description of the girl and the second (BC) to the ardent wooer (with the exception of stanza 2). The description of Nelly is sweet and delicate and she emerges like a woman from a Watteau painting:

> Her closed eyes like weapons sheath'd
>   Were seal'd in soft repose;
> Her lips, still as she fragrant breath'd
>   It richer dy'd the rose.

The tune here (AA), on the other hand, is brisk and energetic and its vitality counterbalances the artificiality of the poem in a refreshing way. The BC-part of the tune is much more agitated: it lies higher, it turns from minor into major and it has more semi-quavers. This gives a kind of physical urgency to the boy's passion and we sense a Burnsian lover behind the pastoral mask:

> Tumultuous tides his pulses roll,
>   A faltering, ardent kiss he stole;
> He gaz'd, he wish'd, he fear'd, he blush'd,
>   And sigh'd his very soul.

The repeated semi-quaver figure with its restlessness in C_1 and C_2 has its counterpart in the phrasal repetition in the refrain ("He gaz'd" etc.), and slightly overdone as it seems when sung, the boy here almost becomes a comic figure in all his passion. In the last half-stanza it is clear that Burns treats the lovers as marionettes in a conventional pastoral play. Line 29 expresses the poet's objective view of the scene and of the convention. Here Burns points out to the listener what he is doing and what is expected of him as a poet: "But Willy follow'd,—as he should, / He overtook her in the wood". Yet he gives the love-making some of that earthy physical quality which we find in the bawdy songs. It is only implied—in the urgency of the tune and in the girl's final surrender—but it is there.

Conclusion

We shall never know quite what kind of expression a Burns song has until it is sung, and only then—when we hear its tempo, its rhythm and its melody—only then will we know its general tenor and only then should we give our judgement on it. The contention in this thesis has been that important dimensions of Burns's songs are lost if the lyrics are severed from their tunes. It may then be asked what these dimensions are. What new expressions do we find in Burns's songs if we consider not only their words but also their music and the interplay between these two elements? From my investigations some conclusions can be drawn, and I have found that there are four aspects of the songs which are closely connected with the expression of the tune: (1) emotion, (2) character, (3) humour, (4) dramatic effect.

Burns's songs are to a large extent emotional songs; most of them express the feelings of happy or unhappy love, but they also sing of other kinds of joys and sorrows. These sentiments may be suggested in the lyric text but they are only given their full gamut of expression in conjunction with the tune. In some songs even, the emotion behind the words lies wholly in the tune and a song like "Jamie come try me" means little without its tune. In Chapter 3 it has been shown how the emotions of young girls in love are revealed through the music in a much more palpable way than had been the case if the songs had only been read: the restlessness and impatience of the girl in "Tam Glen" and the sadness at being oppressed by her parents of the girl in "O, for ane and twenty Tam", the tender and intensive longing in "For the sake o' Somebody", the anguish in "Ay waukin O" and the passion in "Jamie come try me", the happy and uncomplicated feelings of love in "Young Jockey was the blythest lad", the regret in "To the weaver's gin ye go" and the protective love for a child in "Bonie Dundee"—a great variety of emotions, all conveyed or enhanced by the music. As examples from other chapters mention can be made of the grief and despair in "The Banks o' Doon", the tender feelings in "Afton Water" and "John Anderson my Jo", the happiness in "Bonie Bell" and "I'll ay ca' in by yon town" and the exuberance in "The De'il's awa wi' th' Exciseman".

Through the tune also the character of the protagonist in a song may be more vividly conveyed and this is particularly noticeable in the songs about young women. In "Tam Glen" and "I'm o'er young to Marry Yet" the tunes give indications of girlishness and innocence, and in "O, for ane and twenty

131

Tam" it suggests a more mature and independent girl. The girl in "Wha is that at my bower door?" is given a certain strength of character through the tune and in "The rantin dog the Daddie o't" she seems to have a healthy, unworried attitude. In "Tibbie Dunbar", one of the few songs where a young laddie is in the centre, the tune emphasizes his strong and uncompromising character.

The third element which may be better brought forth by musical means is humour. The subtle humour in the dialogue of "Wha is that at my bower door?" or in "Whistle o'er the lave o't" is much more pronounced when sung, the description of the horrible man in "What can a young lassie do wi' an auld man" is made to laugh at and its humour is strengthened by the tune, and the very drastic humour of the situation in "Willie brew'd a peck o' maut" is vividly dramatized by the tune.

In some songs, finally, the tune has a clear dramatic function: it brings out dramatic elements and draws our attention to expressions in the lyric which we may not have noticed without the tune. The unexpectedness of the line "And ay she set the wheel between" in "Duncan Davison", for instance, is much more dramatic when sung, and the climax in "The weary Pund o' Tow" (when the woman breaks the distaff on the man's head) receives much of its impact from the tune. In "Bonie Dundee" the music suggests an action: the young mother looks down on the baby and then away into the distance. In "Then Guidwife count the lawin" the music brings out a switch of attention (from the table to the landlady) and we can more easily experience the situation. In "The De'il's awa wi' th' Exciseman" we can feel the dancing rhythm and in "What can a young lassie do wi' an auld man" almost hear the girl stamping her foot with anger and dancing away at the end.

The analyses of the songs also show that subtleties, of sentiment, of character, of humour, and of action, can be exquisitely expressed by means of music. Many ironic or humorous twists, emotional implications and pictorial effects would be completely lost to a reader of the songs. As examples of this can be mentioned the ambiguous endings in "To the Weaver's gin ye go" and "Green grow the Rashes", the almost anguished happiness in "The bonny wee thing", the rhetorical antitheses and ironic implications of "Whistle o'er the lave o't", the expressive musical descent at the end of "John Anderson my Jo" to accompany the symbolic descent on life's hill, the coming and going of the wind in "Up in the Morning Early", the leitmotif in "Afton Water", and the dramatic effect of the pause after "Scroggam" in the song of the same name.

This recapitulation of different expressive elements in a song thus shows that a deeper understanding of Burns's songs must be based on analyses of both lyric and tune. A neglect of the music will inevitably lessen the impact of any of the four aspects discussed above. It may then be asked what the means are of achieving these joint effects. In Chapter 2 it was claimed that certain relationships exist between the structure, rhythm and melody of the tune on one hand, and the form, metre and mood of the lyric on the other, and my method has been to investigate these three related elements of a song. From this investigation the following conclusions can be drawn: (1) Burns had a fine sense of structure, and the structure of the tune is sometimes used for expressive purposes; (2) rhythm and melody are the main musical means of expression, but there is no clear correspondence between a particular type of rhythm or melody and a particular type of theme.

Examples of Burns's sense of structure and sensitive ear for the organization of the lyric to the musical material are "Jamie come try me", "Wilt thou be my Dearie", "Whistle o'er the lave o't" and "The rantin dog the Daddie o't". The dialogue forms of "Eppie McNab" and "Wha is that at my bower door?" and the return to the introductory theme in the second stanza of "Gloomy December" all show an awareness of the expressive effect of structural devices, as do also the accumulative patterns in "What can a young lassie do wi' an auld man" and "To daunton me".

The two-part structure of most tunes with a lift in the second half nearly always has an effect on the lyric, since the intensification in the lift more or less automatically gives it a new emotional shade. But in several songs Burns makes the lyric expression correspond to this shift by giving it a new tenor in the second half. See for example "Young Jockey was the blythest lad", where the objective description of the boy in the first half and the girl's subjective feelings for him in the second correspond to the melodic and rhythmic shift in the tune. In "Tibbie Dunbar" the boy's declaration of love becomes braver and more provocative in the second half where the tune rises, and in "John Anderson my Jo" the contrast between then and now and young and old is displayed against the shift in the music.

Throughout the thesis I have shown how the main instruments of expression are rhythm and melody, and how these are very flexible tools which adapt themselves to different lyric moods at the same time as they enhance these expressions and bring out new dimensions. The difference between the relaxed lilt of the triple rhythm and the more rigid quadruple rhythm is well illustrated by "Song" ("The gloomy night") and "The lazy mist" which are both gloomy songs, and yet the latter seems much lighter because of its triple rhythm. "Bonie Dundee" and "Afton Water" get their lullaby qualities from the triple rhythm, in "Gloomy December" and "Song" ("Ae fond kiss") it becomes expressive of sighing and in "There'll never be peace till Jamie comes home" of resignation. Triple rhythm is also successfully used for happy songs like "Bonie Bell", dancing songs like "The De'il's awa wi' th' Exciseman" and for playful songs like "We'll hide the Couper behint the door". But such types of songs may also be given their characters by duple or quadruple rhythms as in "Then

Guidwife count the lawin", "Theniel Menzies' bony Mary" and "The birks of Aberfeldey".

The lack of the upbeat is very important in "Wha is that at my bower door?" to emphasize the girl's irritation and in "Robert Bruce's March to Bannockburn" to intensify the force of the exhortations. The snaps become expressive of emotional pain in "The bonny wee thing" and "The Banks o' Doon", of suppressed anger in "What can a young lassie do wi' an auld man", and of drunkenness in "Willie brew'd a peck o' maut". The dotted rhythm emphasizes expressive consonants in "O lay thy loof in mine lass" and "What can a young lassie do wi' an auld man", it brings out the antitheses in "Whistle o'er the lave o't", and it is expressive of the conversational diction of "The weary Pund o' Tow". Undotted rhythm becomes expressive of gentle love in "John Anderson my Jo", "The Gardener wi' his paidle" and "Afton Water" and of light-hearted happiness in "Bonie Bell" and "I'll ay ca' in by yon town". The quick tempo suggested innocence in "Tam Glen" and the slow tempo more self-confidence in "O, for ane and twenty Tam".

A minor mode often emphasizes a sad trait in the lyric as in "O, for ane and twenty Tam" and a major mode gaiety as in "Bonie Bell", "Then Guidwife count the lawin" and many others. High registers intensify as in the stanzas of "O, for ane and twenty Tam" and in "Duncan Davison" and a large melodic range may be expressive of a large emotional range as in "Jamie come try me". Melodic rises express activity and agression in "Wha is that at my bower door?", despair in "Stay, my Charmer, can you leave me", urgency in "Tibbie Dunbar", protest in "There'll never be peace till Jamie comes hame", and exhortation in "Robert Bruce's March to Bannockburn". Leaps bring out significant words like in "Tam Glen" and "Craigieburn-wood" and melodic falls emphasize sadness and despondency in "Gloomy December" and "The Highland widow's lament". The authentic range gives a certain strength and power to "My Harry was a Gallant gay" and the double triad varies the nuances of the girl's voice in "The rantin dog the Daddie o't".

As Burns wrote many of his songs in a traditional style, or took his material from old songs, he also took over certain patterns of this style, patterns which are unmistakably connected with songs to be sung. These formulas are repetitions, refrains, and choruses, and the way Burns has used them for expressive purposes in conjunction with the tune further proves how important it is that his songs are sung.

Burns claimed that he was not very fond of choruses (Letter 580) and only about a fourth of the songs investigated have a chorus. Yet when he used them he had them play an important role in the total expression of the song and therefore, when sung, these choruses give the songs a dimension which they do not have when read—then they may seem rather cumbersome. In "My Harry

134

was a Gallant gay", for instance, the repeated chorus, sung in a higher and more intense register, along with the refrain become expressive of the predominant thought in the girl's mind. In "Ay waukin O" it embodies the girl's longing and in "Jamie come try me" her passion. In "To the Weaver's gin ye go" the chorus is a forewarning and a comment on the girl's words in the stanzas, in "The weary Pund o' Tow" it becomes the almost symbolic reminder of the kind of life described in the song, and in "Craigieburn-wood" the chorus is a reminder of the poet's yearning. In "Then Guidwife count the lawin" the chorus has a dramatic function (there is a switch of attention) and in "The De'il's awa wi' th' Exciseman", "Theniel Menzies' bony Mary" and many others a social one (the people join in the singing).

Refrains and repetitions, like choruses, often have a tedious effect on the printed page, but these devices, when analysed in conjunction with their tunes, are often very expressive, sometimes by very subtle means. Through a change in the music identical lines are given different nuances not to be found in the words only, for instance in "Jamie come try me", "Stay, my Charmer, can you leave me", "O lay thy loof in mine lass", "Eppie McNab", "Tibbie Dunbar" and "Awa whigs awa". In the same way as choruses, refrains and repetitions may emphasize a recurring thought, such as the repetition of the boy's name in "Tam Glen". They may also be expressive of exuberance and joy, as in the refrains of "The De'il's awa wi' th' Exciseman", "The birks of Aberfeldey" and "We'll hide the Couper behint the door".

David Daiches has pointed at the difficulties of the critic of Burns's songs:

The criticism of song lyrics is not easy. The analytic technique which demonstrates subtlety and paradox in the organization is inapplicable to poems which are meant to be sung and which are often written in order to recapture folk emotion. Modern criticism, which does so well with John Donne or an ode of Keats, is singularly ill equipped for an appraisal of Burns's songs. In this venture our only guide can be Arnold's instruction to see the object in itself as it really is, and a determination to account for its appeal as honestly and sensitively as possible.[1]

In this thesis I have suggested what tools can be used to arrive at a just evaluation of the songs, and in my analyses and in the conclusion I have shown with what skill Burns used these tools. I have also pointed to the fact that important aspects of the expression of the songs are either completely lost, or not given their full dimension, if the lyrics are severed from their tunes. It therefore seems obvious that Burns's songs must never be interpreted as lyrical creations only—they are entities composed of both text and tune where one is dependent on the other for its effect.

[1] Daiches, *Robert Burns,* p. 298.

Glossary

The glossary includes only Scots-English words not glossed in the body of the text.

a', *all*
ae, *one; only*
aft(en), *often*
aik, *oak*
ain, *own*
aith, *oath*
amang, *among*
an('), *and; if*
ance, *once*
ane, *one*
anither, *another*
auld, *old*
awa, *away*
awauk, *awake*
behin(t), *behind*
beld, *bald*
blaw, *blow*
blude, *blood*
bluid, *blood*
braid, *broad*
brak, *break*
brust, *burst*
ca', *call*
cam, *came*
canna, *cannot*
cauld, *cold*
compleen, *complain*
daunton, *daunt*
de'il, *devil*
diel, *devil*
dochter, *daughter*
drap, *drop*
e'e, *eye*
een, *eyes*
e'en, *evening*
e'en, *even*
fa', *fall*
fause, *false*
forgie, *forgive*
fou, *full; drunk*
frae, *from*

fu', *full; drunk*
gae, *go; give*
gaed, *went*
gane, *gone*
gang, *go*
gat, *got*
gie, *give*
gif, *if*
gowd, *gold*
gude, *good*
guid, *good*
ha', *hall*
hae, *have*
haly, *holy*
hame, *home*
han', *hand*
haud, *hold*
i', *in*
ither, *other*
laik, *lack*
lan', *land*
lanely, *lonely*
lang, *long*
lawlands, *lowlands*
lippie, dim. of *lip*
lo'e, *love*
mair, *more*
mak, *make*
'mang, *among*
maun, *must*
maut, *malt; ale*
monie, *money*
naebody, *nobody*
naething, *nothing*
nane, *none*
o', *of*
o'er, *over*
o't, *of it*
oursel, *ourselves*
pu', *pull*
pund, *pound*

rash, *rush*
's, *is*
sae, *so*
sair, *sore; sad*
sall, *shall*
sang, *song*
saut, *salt*
sen', *send*
shill, *shrill*
sic, *such*
siller, *silver*
simmer, *summer*
snaw, *snow*
spak, *spoke*
strade, *strode*
tae, *toe*
ta'en, *taken*
tak, *take*
thegither, *together*
thro', *through*
tipence, *twopence*
twa, *two*
'twad, *it would*
wa', *wall*
wad, *would*
wadna, *would not*
wae, *woe*
warld, *world*
wat, *wet*
wauk, *be awake; wake up*
wauken, see wauk
waukin, *awake; sleepless*
weel, *well*
wha, *who*
wham, *whom*
whare, *where*
wi', *with*
winna, *will not*
wrang, *wrong*
ye'se, *you shall*

136

List of Works Quoted or Referred To

Primary Sources and Texts

Manuscripts

Hastie MSS. British Library Add. MS. 22307.

Printed Books

Burns, Robert. *The Letters of Robert Burns.* Ed. J. De Lancey Ferguson. 2 vols. Oxford: Clarendon, 1931.
— *The Merry Muses of Caledonia.* Ed. James Barke and Sidney Goodsir Smith. London: W. H. Allen, 1965.
— *Notes on Scottish Song by Robert Burns: Written in an Interleaved Copy of the Scots Musical Museum with Additions by Robert Riddell and Others.* Ed. James C. Dick. London: Henry Frowde, 1908.
— *The Poems and Songs of Robert Burns.* Ed. James Kinsley. 3 vols. Oxford: Clarendon, 1968.
— *Poems, Chiefly in the Scottish Dialect.* Kilmarnock: John Wilson, 1786.
— *Poems, Chiefly in the Scottish Dialect.* Edinburgh: William Creech, 1787.
— *Poems, Chiefly in the Scottish Dialect.* 2nd enl. ed. 2 vols. Edinburgh: William Creech, 1793.
— *The Poetry of Robert Burns.* Ed. William E. Henley and Thomas F. Henderson. 4 vols. Edinburgh: T. C. and E. C. Jack, 1901.
— *Robert Burns: Selected Poetry and Prose.* Ed. Robert D. Thornton. Boston: Houghton Mifflin, 1966.
— *Robert Burns's Commonplace Book 1783—1785.* Facsimile edition. Ed. James C. Ewing and Davidson Cook. Glasgow: Gowans and Gray, 1938.
— *Robert Burns's Tours of the Highlands and Stirlingshire 1787.* Ed. Raymond Lamont Brown. Ipswich: The Boydell Press, 1973.
— *The Songs of Robert Burns Now First Printed with the Melodies for Which They Were Written: A Study in Tone-Poetry.* Ed. James C. Dick. London: Henry Frowde, 1903.
— *The Tuneful Flame: Songs of Robert Burns as He Sang Them.* Ed. Robert D. Thornton. Kansas: Univ. of Kansas Press, 1957.
Cook, Davidson. "Annotations of Scottish Songs by Burns: An Essential Supplement to Cromek and Dick", *Annual Burns Chronicle and Club Directory,* 31 (1922), 1—21.
The Scots Musical Museum. Ed. James Johnson. 6 vols. Edinburgh, 1787—1803.

The Scots Musical Museum Originally Published by James Johnson with Illustrations of the Lyric Poetry and Music of Scotland by William Stenhouse. Vol. I. 1853, facsimile edition, Hatboro, Pa.: Folklore Associates, 1962.

A Select Collection of Original Scotish Airs for the Voice. Ed. George Thomson. 5 vols. London, 1793—1818.

Secondary Sources

Burns Criticism

Angellier, Auguste. *Étude sur la vie et les œuvres de Robert Burns.* 2 vols. Paris: Librairie Hachette, 1892.

Carswell, Catherine. *The Life of Robert Burns.* London: Chatto & Windus, 1930.

Cook, Davidson. "Burns and old song books", *The Scottish Musical Magazine,* 3, Nos. 8 and 11 (1927), 147—49, 207—09.

— "Burns's 'Oswald': The 'Caledonian Pocket Companion'", *The Scots Magazine,* 19, No. 5 (1933), 372—81.

Crawford, Thomas. *Burns: A Study of the Poems and Songs.* Edinburgh: Oliver and Boyd, 1960.

Daiches, David. *Robert Burns.* 2nd rev. ed. London: André Deutsch, 1966.

— "Robert Burns and Jacobite Song", *Critical Essays on Robert Burns.* Ed. Donald A. Low. London: Routledge, 1975.

Ferguson, J. De Lancey. *Pride and Passion: Robert Burns 1759—1796.* New York: OUP, 1939.

Fitzhugh, Robert T. *Robert Burns: The Man and the Poet. A Round Unvarnished Account.* Boston: Houghton Mifflin, 1970.

Hecht, Hans. *Robert Burns: The Man and His Work.* Trans. Jane Lymburn. 2nd rev. ed. Edinburgh: William Hodge, 1950.

Keith, Alexander. *Burns and Folk-song.* Aberdeen: D. Wyllie & Son, 1922.

Keith, Christina. *The Russet Coat: A Critical Study of Burns' Poetry and of Its Background.* London: Robert Hale, 1956.

Kinsley, James. "The Music of the Heart", *Renaissance and Modern Studies,* 8 (1964), 5—52.

McCourt, Tom M. "The Forgotten Songs of Robert Burns", *Étude Music Magazine,* 69 (1951), 12—13.

Montgomerie, William. "Folk Poetry and Robert Burns", *Burns Chronicle and Club Directory,* 2nd ser., 12 (1950), 21—29.

Ritter, Otto. *Quellenstudien zu Robert Burns 1773—1791.* Palaestra 20. Berlin: Mayer & Müller, 1901.

Snyder, Frank Bliss. *The Life of Robert Burns.* New York: Macmillan, 1932.

— *Robert Burns: His Personality, His Reputation and His Art.* Toronto: Univ. of Toronto Press, 1936.

Thornton, Robert D. "Twentieth-Century Scholarship on the Songs of Robert Burns", *University of Colorado Studies: Series in Language and Literature.* No. 4. Boulder, Col.: Univ. of Col. Press, 1953, pp. 75—92.

Thorpe Davie, Cedric. "Robert Burns, Writer of Songs", *Critical Essays on Robert Burns.* Ed. Donald A. Low. London: Routledge, 1975.

Other Works

Aikin, John. *Essays on Song-Writing: with a collection of such English songs as are most eminent for poetical merit. To which are added some original pieces.* 2nd ed. Warrington: William Eyres, 1774.

Beattie, James. "On Poetry and Music, as they affect the Mind", *Essays.* Edinburgh: William Creech, 1776.

Bronson, Bertrand Harris. *The Ballad as Song.* Berkeley: Univ. of Calif. Press, 1969.

— "Literature and Music", *Relations of Literary Study: Essays on Interdisciplinary Contributions.* Ed. James Thorpe. New York: MLA, 1967.

— "Some Aspects of Music and Literature in the Eighteenth Century", *Music & Literature in England in the Seventeenth and Eighteenth Centuries.* Los Angeles: William Andrews Clark Memorial Library, 1953.

Brown, Calvin S. *Music and Literature: A Comparison of the Arts.* 1948; rpt. Athens, Georgia: The Univ. of Georgia Press, 1949.

Butler, Charles. *The Principles of Music, in Singing and Setting: with the two-fold use thereof, ecclasiasticall and civil.* London: Iohn Haviland, 1636.

The Caledonian Pocket Companion. Ed. James Oswald. 12 vols. London, 1743—59 [dates approximate].

Campbell, Alexander. *An Introduction to the History of Poetry in Scotland from the beginning of the thirteenth century to the present time; with a conversation on Scotish Song . . . To which are subjoined Songs of the lowlands of Scotland.* Edinburgh: Andrew Foulis, 1798.

The Charmer: a choice collection of songs, Scots and English. Edinburgh: I. Yair, 1749.

A Collection of Highland Vocal Airs. Ed. Patrick MacDonald. Edinburgh, 1784 [date approximate].

Collinson, Francis. *The Traditional and National Music of Scotland.* 1966; rpt. London: Routledge, 1970.

Cooke, Deryck. *The Language of Music.* Oxford: OUP, 1959.

Cooper, Grosvenor W. and Meyer, Leonard B. *The Rhythmic Structure of Music.* Chicago: The Univ. of Chicago Press, 1960.

Crawford, Thomas. "Scottish Popular Ballads and Lyrics of the Eighteenth and Early Nineteenth Centuries: Some Preliminary Conclusions", *Studies in Scottish Literature,* 1 (1963), 49—63.

Dabney, Julia P. *The Musical Basis of Verse: A Scientific Study of the Principles of Poetic Composition.* New York: Longmans, Green and Co., 1901.

Daiches, David. *The Paradox of Scottish Culture: The Eighteenth-Century Experience.* London: OUP, 1964.

Dauney, William. *Ancient Scottish Melodies.* Edinburgh: Maitland Club, 1838.

Davison, Archibald T. *Words and Music: A Lecture delivered . . . December 10, 1953.* Washington: Library of Congress, 1954.

Emmerson, George S. *Rantin' Pipe and Tremblin' String: A History of Scottish Dance Music.* London: J. M. Dent, 1971.

Farmer, Henry George. *A History of Music in Scotland.* London: Hinrichsen, 1947.

Greig, Gavin. *Folk-song in Buchan and Folk-song of the North-east.* Hatboro, Pa.: Folklore Associates, 1963.

— "Song-writing", in A. Stephen Wilson. *Words Wooing Music.* Aberdeen: John Rae Smith, 1890.

Gunnyon, William. *Illustrations of Scottish History, Life and Superstition from Song and Ballad.* Glasgow: Robert Forrester, 1879.

Harris, David Fraser. *Saint Cecilia's Hall.* Edinburgh: Oliphant Anderson and Ferrier, 1911.

Hecht, Hans. Ed. *Songs from David Herd's Manuscripts.* Edinburgh: William J. Hay, 1904.

Hendren, J. W. *A Study of Ballad Rhythm: With Special Reference to Ballad Music.* Princeton Studies in English, No. 14. Princeton: Princeton UP, 1936.

Herd, David. Ed. *The Ancient and Modern Scots Songs, heroic ballads, &c. now first collected into one body.* 2nd enl. ed. 2 vols. Edinburgh, 1776.

Hogg, James. Ed. *The Jacobite Relics of Scotland: being songs, airs, and legends of the adherents of the House of Stuart.* 2 vols. Edinburgh: W. Blackwood, 1819–21.

Jack, Ronald D. *The Italian Influence of Scottish Literature.* Edinburgh: Edinburgh UP, 1972.

Johnson, David. *Music and Society in Lowland Scotland in the Eighteenth Century.* London: OUP, 1972.

Karpeles, Maud. *An Introduction to English Folk Song.* London: OUP, 1973.

The Lark: containing a collection of above four hundred and seventy English and Scotch Songs. London, 1740.

Mackenzie, Henry. *The Anecdotes and Egotisms.* Oxford: OUP, 1927.

Maidment, James. Ed. *Scotish Songs and Ballads.* Edinburgh: T. G. Stevenson, 1859.

Nettl, Bruno. *Folk and Traditional Music of the Western Continents.* Englewood Cliffs, N.J.: Prentice-Hall, 1965.

— *Theory and Method in Ethnomusicology.* London: The Free Press of Glencoe, 1964.

Orpheus Caledonius: or, a collection of the best Scotch songs set to musick by W. Thomson. Ed. William Thomson. London, 1725 [date approximate].

Pattison, Bruce. *Music and Poetry of the English Renaissance.* London: Methuen, 1948.

Ramsay, Allan. Ed. *The Tea-Table Miscellany: A Collection of Choice Songs.* Edinburgh, 1723.

Ritson, Joseph. Ed. *A Select Collection of English Songs.* 3 vols. London, 1783.

A Selection of Scotch, English, Irish and Foreign Airs. Ed. James Aird. Vol. III. Glasgow, 1788.

Schueller, Herbert M. "Literature and Music as Sister Arts: An Aspect of Aesthetic Theory in Eighteenth-Century Britain", *Philological Quarterly,* 26, No. 3 (1947), 193–205.

Sharp, Cecil J. *English Folk Song: Some Conclusions.* 4th ed., rev. Maud Karpeles, 1965; rpt. London: EP Publishing Ltd., 1972.

Shuldham-Shaw, P. N. and Lyle, E. B. Ed. "Folk-Song in the North-East: J. B. Duncan's Lecture, 1908", *Scottish Studies,* 18 (1974), 1–37.

Sonnenschein, Edward A. *What is Rhythm?* Oxford: Basil Blackwell, 1925.

Stein, Jack M. *Poem and Music in the German Lied from Gluck to Hugo Wolf.* Cambridge, Mass.: Harvard UP, 1971.

Tytler, William. "A Dissertation on the Scottish Music", in Hugo Arnot. *The History of Edinburgh from the Earliest Accounts to the Present Time.* Edinburgh, 1779.

Walker, Ernest. *A History of Music in England.* 3rd rev. and enl. ed. Oxford: Clarendon, 1952.

Wittig, Kurt. *The Scottish Tradition in Literature.* Edinburgh: Oliver and Boyd, 1958.

Index of Songs

The index includes short titles and first lines of songs and choruses.